Great Teaching by Design

Great Teaching by Design

From Intention to Implementation in the **Visible Learning®** Classroom

John Hattie
Vince Bustamante
John Almarode
Douglas Fisher
Nancy Frey

CORWIN
A SAGE Publishing Com

FOR INFORMATION:

Corwin

A SAGE Company

2455 Teller Road

Thousand Oaks, California 91320

www.corwin.com

SAGE Ltd.

1 Oliver's Yard

55 City Road

London, EC1Y 1SP

United Kingdom

SAGE Pvt. Ltd.

B 1/I 1 Mohan Cooperative Industrial Area

Mathura Road, New Delhi 110 044

India

SAGE Publications Asia-Pacific Pte. Ltd.

18 Cross Street #10-10/11/12

China Square Central

Singapore 048423

Acquisitions Editor: Jessica Allan

Senior Development Editor: Lucas Schleicher

Associate Development Editor: Mia Rodriguez

Production Editor: Veronica Stapleton Hooper

Copy Editor: Gretchen Treadwell

Typesetter: Hurix Digital

Proofreader: Dennis W. Webb

Indexer: Integra

Cover Designer: Candice Harman

Marketing Manager: Maura Sullivan

Printed in the United States of America

Library of Congress Cataloging-in-Publication Data

Names: Hattie, John, author. | Bustamante, Vince, author. | Almarode, John, author. | Fisher, Douglas, 1965- author. | Frey, Nancy, 1959- author.

Title: Great teaching by design : from intention to implementation in the visible learning classroom / John Hattie, Vince Bustamante, John Almarode, Douglas Fisher, Nancy Frey.

Description: Thousand Oaks, California : Corwin Press, 2021. | Includes bibliographical references and index.

Identifiers: LCCN 2020033498 | ISBN 9781071818336 (paperback) | ISBN 9781071818343 (epub) | ISBN 9781071818329 (epub) | ISBN 9781071818299 (ebook)

Subjects: LCSH: Effective teaching—United States. | Teacher effectiveness—United States. | Teachers—Training of—United States. | Teachers—In service training—United States.

Classification: LCC LB1025.3 .H3798 2021 | DDC 371.1020973—dc23

LC record available at https://lccn.loc.gov/2020033498

This book is printed on acid-free paper.

SUSTAINABLE FORESTRY INITIATIVE
Certified Chain of Custody
Promoting Sustainable Forestry
www.sfiprogram.org
SFI-01268

20 21 22 23 24 10 9 8 7 6 5 4 3 2 1

CONTENTS

CHAPTER 1

CHAPTER 2

CHAPTER 3

CHAPTER 4

CHAPTER 5

Note from the Publisher: The authors have provided video and web content throughout the book which is available to you through QR Codes. To read a QR Code, you must have a smartphone or tablet with a camera. We recommend that you download a QR Code reader app that is made specifically for your phone or tablet brand.

TABLES, FIGURES, AND QR CODES

CHAPTER 4

CHAPTER 5

ACKNOWLEDGMENTS

From Vince Bustamante

Leading a team of brilliant minds was a daunting task for my first book project, and would not have been possible without the mentorship and guidance of John Almarode. John, thank you so much for your advice, direction, and conversation as we navigated through the creation of this book. Your mentorship has been invaluable. It has been such a pleasure working with you and learning from you. I feel so fortunate to have developed a friendship along the way.

Doug, Nancy, and John H., thank you for your sage advice, thought-provoking questions, and brilliant feedback. It was so reassuring knowing you were always being accessible for calls, emails, and texts. This project has been the best learning of my career, and would not have been nearly as impactful without having you on the team.

Thank you to the editorial team at Corwin, especially Jessica Allan for all of your guidance in bringing this book together. A special thanks goes to Ariel Curry for your encouragement and support (over an In-N-Out milkshake) to bring this project idea forward and help make it a reality.

This book was inspired by the countless teachers and students I have worked with over the course of my career, some even in conversation as this book was being developed. My time working directly with teachers and students has easily been the most enjoyable and inspiring aspect of my career.

Finally, I would like to thank my wife, Leah. You are my rock and greatest support. Thank you for your patience and confidence in me. Having you as my partner has singlehandedly made me a better person and has improved my life immeasurably. I am so lucky to walk beside you through life. Thank you.

From John Almarode

To move from potential to implementation in the classroom requires teachers, teacher leaders, and instructional leaders to work collaboratively with colleagues to leverage the individual expertise and efficacy of each individual. Unpacking a framework for supporting this process also requires collaboration between colleagues. This book represents that collective effort. I am fortunate to work with incredible colleagues who challenge and push my thinking forward. John H., Vince, Doug, and Nancy, thank you for your willingness to engage in critical conversations and dialogue around implementing what works best in teaching and learning. John H., thank you for sharing the DIIE model with us and allowing us to unpack the framework in the pages of this book.

At James Madison University, I am blessed to work with some of the best and brightest students, who one day, in the not so distant future, will turn their own potential into high-quality, high-impact, teaching and learning. I could fill the pages of any book with their names and specific contributions to my own personal and professional journey in education. For now, a heartfelt thank you will have to suffice. Your contributions in class and the hallways of Memorial Hall provide the foundation on which this work is built.

My two children, Tessa and Jackson, provide the motivation to do what I do. You are true blessings and I thank you for your patience and willingness to help daddy think through what works best in teaching and learning. Your lives are better because you spent time in classrooms where teaching was not by chance, but by design.

And last, but certainly not least, I want to thank my wife, Dani. I am still married after yet another book project. Your support is amazing and unyielding. I am grateful you are my wife and even more grateful that we are partners in life. Thank you.

Publisher's Acknowledgments

Corwin wishes to acknowledge the following peer reviewers for their editorial insight and guidance.

Timothy P. Cusack, EdD
Edmonton Catholic Schools
Edmonton, Alberta

Nicole Lafreniere
Edmonton Catholic Schools
Edmonton, Alberta

Brandon Pachan
Peel District School Board
Brampton, Ontario

ABOUT THE AUTHORS

John Hattie, PhD, is an award-winning education researcher and best-selling author with nearly 30 years of experience examining what works best in student learning and achievement. His research, better known as Visible Learning, is a culmination of nearly 30 years synthesizing more than 1,500 meta-analyses comprising more than 90,000 studies involving over 300 million students around the world. He has presented and keynoted in over 350 international conferences and has received numerous recognitions for his contributions to education. His notable publications include *Visible Learning, Visible Learning for Teachers, Visible Learning and the Science of How We Learn, Visible Learning for Mathematics, Grades K–12*, and, most recently, *10 Mindframes for Visible Learning.*

Vince Bustamante is an instructional coach, curriculum content developer, and author who currently works for Edmonton Catholic Schools as a social studies curriculum consultant. Holding an MEd from the University of Victoria (Canada) in Curriculum and Instruction, he serves to incorporate research into classroom practice. As a certified Visible Learning Plus consultant, he is passionate about assessment, teacher clarity, and creating classroom environments that foster deep learning experiences where teachers understand and evaluate their impact on student learning. Twitter: @Vincebusta.

John Almarode, PhD, is an associate professor and executive director of teaching and learning in the College of Education at James Madison University (JMU). He works with pre-service teachers at JMU and actively pursues his research interests. He and his colleagues have presented their work to the United States Congress, the United States Department of Education as well as the Office of Science and Technology Policy at the White House. He has authored multiple articles, reports, book chapters, and over a dozen books on effective teaching and learning in today's schools and classrooms.

Douglas Fisher, **PhD**, is professor of educational leadership at San Diego State University and a leader at Health Sciences High and Middle College. He has served as a teacher, language development specialist, and administrator in public schools and nonprofit organizations, including 8 years as the director of Professional Development for the City Heights Collaborative, during a time of increased student achievement in some of San Diego's urban schools. He has engaged in professional learning communities for several decades, building teams that design and implement systems to impact teaching and learning. He has published numerous books on teaching and learning, such as *The Distance Learning Playbook* and *Engagement by Design*.

Nancy Frey, **PhD**, is a professor in educational leadership at San Diego State University and a leader at Health Sciences High and Middle College. She has been a special education teacher, reading specialist, and administrator in public schools. She has engaged in professional learning communities as a member and in designing schoolwide systems to improve teaching and learning for all students. She has published numerous books, including *The Teacher Clarity Playbook* and *Rigorous Reading*.

INTRODUCTION

This is a book about implementation. Implementation is a critical part of maximizing and accelerating the impact educators have on students' learning. The process of implementation involves turning good ideas into high-impact learning experiences that propel student learning. However, we cannot have implementation without

- Knowing where our learners are in their learning journey
- Knowing what works best in teaching and learning
- Evaluating our impact on student learning

Implementation plays out in the decisions educators make during teaching and learning. Great teaching requires great decision making in face-to-face, hybrid, or remote learning environments. What separates highly effective teachers from others in our profession is their ability to make the right decision, at the right time, for the right experience with their learners (Berliner, 2001). To an outside observer, often an administrator, colleague, or parent, this decision making is perceived to be in the hardwiring of that specific teacher. This is reflected in comments such as, "Mrs. Cross is a natural," "Mr. Sonjay just has a way about him," or "Ms. DeSoto makes it look so easy."

Although these statements are meant as compliments, they suggest that the practice of teaching and the resulting impact on student learning is something you either have or you don't. An often-held belief is that our DNA, and the probabilistic outcomes of our genetics, results in some being hardwired to be highly effective, and others not so much. Let's visit two classrooms that illustrate this point.

Our story begins with Oscar Vasquez and Katherine Meyer. These two teachers are separated by five steps. Five steps are all that is required to walk from Mr. Vasquez's classroom to Ms. Meyer's classroom at South Houston Middle School. However, there are striking differences in these two classrooms. Some are visible to a casual observer and others require closer inspection. The casual observer would quickly notice that the five steps across the seventh-grade hallway reveal a world in which learners are engaged compared with a situation where students simply endure the class period. In one classroom, learners are committed to the task at hand whereas in the other, learners are simply compliant. In one, learners are engaged in authentic experiences but in the other, students are tasked with artificial exercises. As a result of this

> The process of implementation involves turning good ideas into high-impact learning experiences that propel student learning.

five-step transition, the gap between Mr. Vasquez's impact—including cognitive, social-emotional, and behavioral outcomes—and Ms. Meyer's extends well beyond five steps. Visitors are likely to attribute the success of Mr. Vasquez to an innate ability and chalk up Ms. Meyer's classroom to the fact that "she simply doesn't have it." But what if the difference between these two teachers is that Mr. Vasquez simply knows more about teaching and learning than Ms. Meyer?

The five steps, yes wide strides, can be summed up as one teacher who knows where the learners are, knows what works best in teaching and learning, and undertakes continuous evaluation of the teacher's impact on student learning. This approach to teaching and learning is not built into the DNA before one becomes a teacher, not handed down by genetics, but something deliberately learned and clearly applied by one South Houston middle school teacher. One has the skills to implement what works best and the other walks to a different beat. The phrases "approach to teaching and learning" or "skills to implement" look beyond knowing what works best, recognizing that this knowledge still requires implementation in any teaching and learning environment.

The World Knows a Lot About Teaching and Learning

Research, recommendations, and reflections on "good teaching" are everywhere and are widely accessible to all of us. Teachers, instructional coaches, and instructional leaders can become overwhelmed by the abundance of professional resources available on almost any aspect of teaching and learning. As more teachers and learners incorporate remote learning into their educational experience, the number of platforms, tools, and approaches to hybrid and remote learning is increasing at rapid rate as well. Almost all of the approaches, strategies, platforms, and tools to teaching and learning in any environment that are recommended in books, articles, online resources, and professional conferences provide evidence that they work. Thus, when asked "what works," the answer seems to be everything! We need look no further than teachers' own bookshelves to find resources about an approach to teaching that promises to improve student learning. Even more so, a quick search of the Internet provides an even more overwhelming number of links to learning success. So how do we sort through this volume of information?

Research has provided incredible insight into teaching and learning. As it turns out, we know a lot about teaching and learning. From Brophy (1998) to Marzano (2017), Saphier, Haley-Speca, & Gower (2018) to Strong (2018), there is a compelling body of evidence related to school-level, teacher-level, and student-level factors that have a positive influence on student learning. For example, activating prior knowledge, classroom discourse, higher-order questioning, and effective feedback are factors identified as having a positive influence on student learning (e.g., Brophy, 1998; Strong, 2018). The research on learning intentions or objectives and specific learning strategies (e.g., jigsaw, cooperative learning strategies, note-taking, summarizing, deliberate practice, to name a few) suggests that these are effective, value-added tools to improve student learning. With so many "things" that seem to work in face-to-face, hybrid, and remote learning environments, how do educators sort through this ever-growing pile of evidence to make daily decisions that truly impact learning in our classrooms?

Let's return to the classrooms of Mr. Vasquez and Ms. Meyer. When engaging in dialogue about teaching and learning with these teachers, the conversations are very similar. They both talk about having clear learning goals, using assessments, communicating high expectations, keeping learners engaged, establishing rules and procedures conducive for supporting learning, and establishing strong and positive relationships with learners. Both independently assert that they strive for their learners to develop both knowledge and skills that will support them in their lifelong endeavors. Their list includes a number of evidence-based practices that are the foundation for what Marzano (2017) refers to as "the art and science of teaching."

But even when we identify high-impact strategies there is a lot of variation in the effectiveness of certain strategies. Consider the flipped classroom. Mr. Vasquez is an avid reader and has what he calls his "educational reading list" that he works through during the school year and during holidays. He noticed recently that flipped learning has an effect size of 0.56. Interestingly enough, he saw another reference to flipped learning with an effect size of 0.19. Even if we are not experts in interpreting effect sizes, we still recognize that these two values are quite different. What could explain this variation findings? This average effect size of 0.56 is from 20 meta-analyses, but when we look at each meta-analysis separately, we notice averages ranging from 0.19 to 1.19 standard deviations. Again, how do we explain such findings, such differences? Then answer: implementation. This variation reflects the many meanings that teachers make when implementing flipped learning—some provide the PowerPoint, or lecture on video for students to watch before class, some then repeat these in class, or use problems—and this variation is a major reason for these very different effects. Choosing a high-probability intervention is but the first important step; the quality of implementation then matters a lot. Let's take a closer look at effect sizes to help make sense of Mr. Vasquez's challenge in deciding to implement flipped learning.

Choosing a high-probability intervention is but the first important step, the quality of implementation then matters a lot.

Hattie and Zierer's *Visible Learning Insights* (2019) research suggests that approximately 96 percent of everything we do in teaching and learning has a positive influence on student learning. Unfortunately, some of the things that "work" have very little impact on learning whereas other things are much more powerful. By pure chance, Ms. Meyer might select an approach that is supported by evidence. But she might not. We subscribe to the belief that teachers can intentionally design learning experiences for students, selecting tools that should work best, work to implement those tools, and then determining the impact of their decisions.

Posner (2004) described a similar problem to having so many influences on teaching and learning when he explored the overwhelming number of curriculum resources available on the market. From reading curriculum, mathematics programs, STEM kits, and character-building interventions, there is a lot for sale that advertises their effectiveness. Posner recognized the side effects of this situation. He identified three possible outcomes associated with this feeling of being overwhelmed with resources that also apply to the number of research-based instructional interventions, including the following:

1. Disregard the evidence and just use your own intuition or common sense. This is truly teaching by chance.

2. Pick your favorite approach to teaching and learning and use that one approach in your classes. This may not be effective for all learners; thus some learning is left to chance.

3. Borrow from all perspectives on teaching and learning to compose what is often referred to as a bag of tricks. Without determining the impact of these decisions, teaching is left to chance.

Each of these three outcomes contain an element of chance, which we find problematic. Mrs. Meyer could easily close her classroom door and take a chance with her intuition. She could just as easily pick one way of "doing business" and use this approach over and over, taking a chance that it will work every time for every student. Knowing a lot about teaching and learning, and knowing what works, does not naturally lead to effective teaching and learning, especially when overwhelmed by the sheer volume of information available.

To move from *what works* to *what works best*, educators must consider the magnitude of the impact. This magnitude is represented by the average effect size associated with a particular influence, strategy, or approach. The barometer of influence provides a visual representation of effect sizes.

A complete list of influences can be found on Visible Learning MetaX (https://www.visiblelearningmetax.com/), which updates effect sizes regularly.

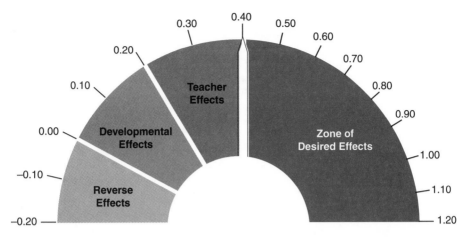

Source: Hattie, J. (2012). *Visible learning for teachers: Maximizing impact on learning. New York, NY*: Routledge.

The effect size serves as a guide for the magnitude of the impact. In this database, the hinge point of 0.40 is average and thus anything with an effect size above 0.40 is above the average and should serve to accelerate learning. Thus, educators can consider approaches to teaching and learning through the lens of which ones have the potential to accelerate learning.

By analyzing the various influences and navigating through the barometer of influences, teachers can truly begin to consider their impact on student learning—a key to becoming a better practitioner.

These influences certainly help guide the decisions Mr. Vasquez, Mrs. Meyer, and all of us make as we answer the question "What works best?" Yet, these effective practices are easily identified by any observer of Mr. Vasquez's classroom and appear to be completely missing from Ms. Meyer's classroom. Yes, you could simply check each of them off the list in one classroom and find no evidence of them in the other. Knowing a lot about teaching and learning does not necessarily mean that people are able to use that knowledge, generate ideas, and then transfer those ideas into their instruction.

What Works Best Is Only Part of the Story

We still have not resolved the relatively common challenge Mr. Vasquez and Ms. Meyer illustrate. There must be more to teaching and learning than simply selecting approaches above the hinge point of 0.40. After all, Mr. Vasquez and Ms. Meyer selected the same influences, strategies, and approaches but realized very different results. Approaches above the hinge point of 0.40 represent the possibility of moving learning forward, yet these approaches still require successful implementation. Even if educators use the barometer of influence to guide decision making,

> By analyzing the various influences and navigating through the barometer of influences, teachers can truly begin to consider their impact on student learning—a key to becoming a better practitioner.

> Approaches above the hinge point of 0.40 represent the possibility of moving learning forward, yet these approaches still require successful implementation.

relying on what works best, the learning outcomes may still be a matter of chance.

We are still not asking the most important question, which is the essential question of this book. Notice that the previous discussion focused on knowing what to do and not on how to do it. Mr. Vasquez and Ms. Meyer did not differ on what they knew about teaching and learning. They differed on their ability to transfer, or implement, that knowledge into high-impact instruction in the specific context of their teaching and learning. So, finally, maybe we have the answer we are looking for. The answer that helps Ms. Meyer and the rest of us accelerate and maximize our impact on student learning is not what works or simply what works best, but instead to ask, *how do we implement what works best?*

Good Ideas Are Not the Same as Implementation

When Fisher, Frey, and Hattie (2016) penned the sentence, "Every student deserves a great teacher, not by chance, but by design" (p. 1), they propelled the role of the decisions teachers make to the forefront of high-impact teaching and learning. The decisions that teachers make each and every day have the *potential* to impact student learning. However, this potential must then be consistently and reliably converted into effective *implementation*. The intention to have an impact on student learning in any learning environment will most assuredly fall short without effective implementation. Knowing what works best in teaching and learning is only part of the story. Taking what we know about what works best in teaching, ensuring effective implementation, and monitoring our impact are what it takes to accomplish the goal of great teaching by design.

> The decisions that teachers make each and every day have the *potential* to impact student learning. However, this potential must then be consistently and reliably converted into effective *implementation*.

Figure I.1 From potential to implementation

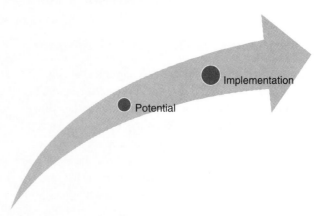

In other words, we must move from the good ideas we have about teaching and learning to the design of a great learning experience to, finally, the implementation of that learning experience in a face-to-face, hybrid, or remote learning context. This book emerged from the challenge to close the gap between potential and implementation.

From Potential to Implementation

Treating the research on teaching and learning as potential tools that can impact student learning above and beyond one year's worth of growth, this book will analyze a process for turning good ideas into high-impact learning experiences that move student learning forward. Selecting approaches with the intention of impacting student learning is only part of the story.

To ensure that learning occurs, we must implement approaches at the right time, with the right content, for the learners in our classroom. Mr. Vasquez and Ms. Meyer may select influences, strategies, and approaches that have the potential to impact their students' learning growth and achievement. And knowing both of these teachers, they made these selections with intention. *The essential difference between Mr. Vasquez and Ms. Meyer is their implementation.* In other words, Mr. Vasquez has implemented specific influences, strategies, and approaches at the right time, with the right content, using the right context (i.e., face-to-face, hybrid, or remote) for his students. Activating prior knowledge, classroom discourse, higher-order questioning, and effective feedback all have the potential to impact student learning above and beyond one year's worth of growth. The use of jigsaw, cooperative learning strategies, note-taking, summarizing, and deliberate practice have the potential to move student learning forward. Successful

Figure I.2 The role of intention in connecting potential and implementation

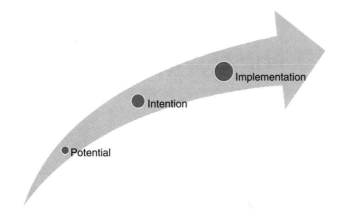

Successful
implementation of these
tools will determine if
that potential is realized
through the visible
impact on student
learning.

implementation of these tools will determine if that potential is realized through the visible impact on student learning.

This is much easier said than done. And we aim to take on this challenge. We aim to promote great teaching, not by chance, but by design. Thus, the intentions of this book are to

- Move from intention to implementation in our teaching and our students' learning.

- Monitor this implementation by continuously gathering evidence of our impact.

To accomplish the intentions of this book, we have to engage in evaluative thinking about our teaching and learning. Whether Mr. Vasquez, Ms. Meyer, and any of their colleagues are in their first year or their twenty-first year of their career, how they approach the decisions they make about teaching and learning should involve these four critical components of evaluative thinking:

1. Discovering where our learners are in their learning journey and where they need to go next in that journey. Where students are in their learning journey represents their learning potential and our teaching potential.

2. Planning, designing, and implementing learning experiences based on the specific context of our classrooms and learners. This planning must focus on the intentional selection of interventions or approaches to teaching and learning.

3. Using evidence-based approaches to teaching and learning that support learners as they move forward in their learning journey. Not only do we identify these evidence-based approaches, but we have to implement them in our teaching and learning.

4. Evaluating the impact of these learning experiences. We must make decisions based on this impact.

There is no doubt that teachers instinctively want to do what is best for their students. As demands and expectations of teachers increase, so does their responsibility to engage in practices that yield the highest student success. As educational practitioners, we must engage in strategies that can both promote student success and ensure teachers do not burn out. "Since it is now widely accepted that teacher quality is a critical component of a successful education, it is clear that much of the burden of meeting these new demands will fall on teachers" (Darling-Hammond & Oakes, 2019, p. 3).

What to Expect in This Book

The purpose of this book is to guide readers through the process of assimilating pedagogical knowledge, content knowledge, and beliefs about teaching and learning to maximize the impact on student learning in all educational environments. The same process that assimilates these elements into high-quality, high-impact teaching in a brick and mortar classroom is the same process that maximizes our teaching in a remote learning environment. What to expect from this book is the answer to the question, *how do we implement what works best?* Let's take the challenge to close the gap between potential, intention, and implementation. Great teaching can be designed, and when it's designed well, students learn more.

"

Highly effective teachers engage in deliberate
decision making, resulting from the specific
ways they think about teaching and learning.

1

CHAPTER 1

IMPLEMENTING WHAT
WORKS BEST

Mr. Salvador is a fourth-grade teacher entering his third year at Maggie Walker Elementary School. His classroom is always active with students engaged in authentic tasks and academic discourse about their learning. His colleagues often comment on his ability to connect with students, motivating them to take on challenging tasks in every content area. Mr. Salvador's learners have demonstrated incredible growth in reading, writing, and mathematics. When asked about his learners' incredible success, he quickly points out that, "my students teach me at the same time I am teaching them." This is evident in the way constructive criticism, reflective questioning, and collaboration are part of the daily learning environment. Mr. Salvador sees learning through the eyes of his students, and his students see themselves as active participants in their own learning. This dynamic between each member of this learning community both informs and guides how to implement what works best in moving learning forward for each learner, regardless of his or her unique characteristics, dispositions about learning, or motivations to learn. Mr. Salvador is an educator who understands how to implement what works best for students.

We *implement what works best* by explicitly uncovering where our learners are in their learning journey, drawing what works best in teaching and learning from the researched evidence of what works best, and continuously evaluating the impact of our decisions on student learning. This process lends itself to an intentional, deliberate, and purposeful approach to implementation that we refer to as the DIIE model (see Figure 1.1). This model is composed of four components that leverage evaluative thinking in teaching and learning. *Diagnosing* or *discovering* where students are in the learning journey directly leads to decisions about what learning *intervention* has the best potential for moving learning forward.

Figure 1.1 The DIIE model

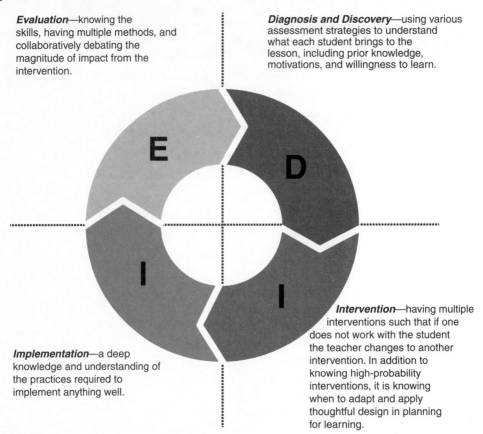

Evaluation—knowing the skills, having multiple methods, and collaboratively debating the magnitude of impact from the intervention.

Diagnosis and Discovery—using various assessment strategies to understand what each student brings to the lesson, including prior knowledge, motivations, and willingness to learn.

Implementation—a deep knowledge and understanding of the practices required to implement anything well.

Intervention—having multiple interventions such that if one does not work with the student the teacher changes to another intervention. In addition to knowing high-probability interventions, it is knowing when to adapt and apply thoughtful design in planning for learning.

The DIIE model is a framework that provides a shared language of teaching and learning for all of us to capitalize on the collective teacher efficacy in all learning environments, the belief that we have an impact on our students' learning and we have the evidence to support that belief. Whether operating in a brick and mortar classroom or through a remote learning environment, this framework supports the implementation of *what works best.*

From there, we must *implement* that intervention through engaging and rigorous learning experiences. And then, we must *evaluate* the impact our decisions had in moving learning forward. The results of that evaluation of impact take us right back to our understanding of where learners are *now* in their learning journey.

The DIIE Model as Shared Language for Implementation

The DIIE model is a framework that provides a shared language of teaching and learning; it allows all of us to capitalize on the collective teacher efficacy in all learning environments, with the belief that we have an impact on our students' learning and evidence to support that belief. The four stages of the DIIE model (diagnosis/discovery, intervention, implementation and evaluation) provide guidance as we engage in turning good ideas into high-impact learning experiences that move student learning forward.

Diagnosis/Discovery. Think back to those first few weeks of school. They seem to fly by with culture-building activities, assemblies, protocol meetings, establishing routines and procedures, and so forth. In those weeks, how are teachers taking time to learn about the dispositions that students bring into the class? It is so easy to get bogged down in the *what of teaching*, frantically planning lessons that link to essential curricular objectives and making sure we have our lesson plans in order. Evaluative thinking strategies challenge teachers to not think of the *what* but of the *who*. Our students: they are the most important determinants in our teaching.

While many teachers spend their time figuring out what to teach, teachers who apply evaluative thinking skills are busy learning about who they will be teaching and what each student brings into the classroom or learning environment. The first component of evaluative thinking ensures that teachers are critically thinking about where their learners are in their learning journey and where to go next in that journey. Where students are in their learning journey represents their learning potential and our teaching potential. This is the focus of the *diagnosis/discovery* component of the DIIE model. When teachers take measures to determine what dispositions, unique characteristics, experiences, and learning opportunities students bring to the learning environment, their teaching practices have the potential to make a greater impact.

Although the DIIE model uses the term "diagnosis" as a descriptor, it should be noted that we do not imply medical diagnoses. Instead, we suggest that teachers take measures to discover (diagnose) more about their learners *before* they attempt to teach content, skills, and understandings. For example, assume you were having a staff dinner party to celebrate the end of a school year. A logical step before cooking would be to ask the staff about any food-related allergies or dietary requirements. Discovering those will allow for a more personalized and inclusive menu for all eaters, and will naturally lead to a better experience for all attendees. By using various assessment strategies to determine what students bring to class, we can be more impactful with our teaching to cater to the specific dispositions of our students.

Intervention. When teachers take appropriate measures to discover who their learners are, they can then move onto the second component of the DIIE model, *intervention*. Understanding the usefulness of interventions when coupled with appropriate knowledge of who our students are as learners is fundamental to ensuring maximum impact on student learning. When the first component in the DIIE model is overlooked, interventions may generate a positive response with students but still may not have the greatest impact. In other words, we do not maximize the potential we have with our learners. Because there are so many learning interventions available to us, it becomes increasingly difficult to sift through the list and determine which have the greatest potential to impact students' learning at this particular moment in their learning progression. Remember, almost everything works but your task is to identify what works best. We should be planning, designing, and implementing learning experiences based on the specific context of our learning environment and learners. This context absolutely includes whether we are in a face-to-face classroom or a remote learning environment. This planning must focus on the intentional selection of an intervention or approach to teaching and learning.

Although the key to successful intervention lies in thorough discovery of student dispositions, unique characteristics, previous experiences, and learning opportunities, there is also a thoughtful process needed to incorporate specific interventions in your teaching and learning. Teachers must not only seek out high-impact approaches, they should also understand there is a time and a place for using these approaches (Hattie & Donoghue, 2016). In order to successfully select interventions, teachers should consider:

1. Do we have multiple interventions available to us? (in case, with some students, the first does not work)

2. Do we know when to apply these interventions?

3. Do we know when to adapt or make changes to the intervention based on what we know about our learners?

Implementation. The third component of the DIIE model, *implementation,* is just as significant as having access to high-impact interventions. When we seek out evidence-based approaches to teaching and learning we can support our learners as they move forward in their learning journey—but only if we implement those approaches in an effective way.

Due to the abundance of strategies and interventions available, we tend to experience information overload about which strategy or intervention to use and when. Think of a time a professional resource was passed along for your consideration and use by colleagues. Often, these resources were recommended to you because your colleague experienced some level of success in implementing this resource with his or her own learners. While it is fantastic your colleague has found ways to implement this approach, strategy, or idea in way that yields a positive impact on student learning, you must consider two things: (1) the local context of your own learning environment (face-to-face, hybrid, or virtual), and (2) the adaptations necessary to make this approach, strategy, or idea successful within your local context.

The implementation process must ensure that evidence-based approaches (i.e., interventions) are clear to all stakeholders (e.g., students, teachers, parents) and vary in both applicability and task. These interventions would not only need to be identified but also implemented with fidelity to ensure our students make progress in their learning journey. Teachers should thus use a critical or evaluative lens when considering this stage. Implementation means knowing when to use certain interventions at certain times of the learning process.

Evaluation. We will never really be able to "know thy impact" on student learning without the evaluation of our practice. This must be done in collaboration with our colleagues or our learners. The final component in the DIIE model, *evaluation* tasks us with looking at the implementation of teaching strategies to determine the impact our decisions around interventions and implementation had on student growth and progress. As we evaluate our impact, we should note there is a distinct difference between student progress and student achievement. To truly implement teaching strategies equitably, students must be aware of their own growth and progress, as well as the overall expectations of their learning outcomes. These outcomes include academic, behavioral, and social-emotional outcomes.

Successful evaluation of impact requires us to think back to the beginning of the DIIE model and really consider our initial decision making. While this may sound like a large philosophical consideration, we must keep the impact on our students' learning as the central focus. During the evaluation component of the DIIE model, we have to reflect on our previous decisions and determine where we are going next in our teaching and students' learning. As we reflect, we should know the expected impact of these learning experiences on our learners.

However, the DIIE model is much more complex than a step-by-step list or prescription that teachers can check off or administer. The decisions each component of the model prompts are situated in ways of thinking and motivations (see Figure 1.2).

There are two sayings that come to mind here: how we feel is real; it is the link to how we think and where the mind goes the person follows. Although a bit cliché, these sayings highlight to role of beliefs, or ways of thinking, and motivations in our decision making. Our beliefs about teaching and learning drive our decisions about implementation. Our motivation for deciding to pursue a career in teaching influences our decisions about implementation. Implementing what works best cannot be discussed in the absence

Implementing what works best cannot be discussed in the absence of beliefs and motivations.

Figure 1.2 DIIE is situated in our ways of thinking and motivations

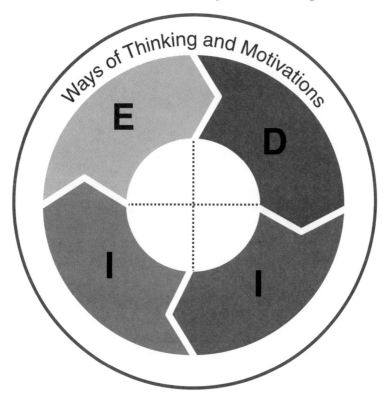

of beliefs and motivations. Let's look at what we know about how beliefs and motivations are highly predictive of implementing what works best.

Ways of Thinking and Motivations

Justin Booth is a middle school science teacher who by most any measure (e.g., student growth, student–teacher relationships, content knowledge, pedagogical content knowledge, etc.) would be identified as a highly effective teacher. He greets learners as they enter the classroom, eager to get started on their entrance tickets. "I want to make sure we are ready to go with the day's learning. The entrance ticket helps students pull together their prior knowledge and, at the same time, gives me insight into what they already know about today's topic."

As learners complete their entrance tickets, Mr. Booth moves through the room checking in on learners with questions about their entrance tickets as well as personal questions. Savannah, a student in Mr. Booth's classroom, shares that "Mr. Booth always asks me about soccer practice, and then, will give me feedback on my work in the same sentence. He really cares and makes me feel like I matter."

After a very specific amount of time, Mr. Booth stops his learners and asks them to take a look at the day's learning intention and success criteria. "Folks, based on your responses on the entrance ticket, I believe we will need to spend a little more time on describing the differences between independent and dependent variables. No problem! We will take care of it, for sure." Without any hesitation, he then jumps right into the day's learning. There are several things that stand out in this classroom. In addition to the above snapshot, Mr. Booth brings the characteristics of an expert teacher to life with the following:

- Providing a cohesive and caring learning community that includes collaboration among and between peers

- Maximizing instructional time through engaging learning experiences or tasks

- Recognizing that classroom management is a process for establishing an effective learning environment

- Aligning his planning, instruction, and assessment to what learners are expected to know, understand, and be able to do in his eighth-grade science classroom

- Establishing clarity for learning through learning intentions, success criteria, and sharing that information with his learners

- Presenting content, weaving in skills, and bringing understanding through a clear structure and connections

- Implementing academic discourse through planned questioning to elicit and conceptualize student learning

- Offering opportunities for deliberate practice that is supported by feedback

- Scaffolding learning to ensure equity in access and opportunity to learning

- Monitoring student learning through a variety of checks for understanding (adapted from Brophy, 1998)

To gain insight into how teachers like Mr. Booth take good ideas and turn them into successful implementation, we have to look inside the face-to-face classrooms or remote learning environments of teachers who do this on a regular basis. Highly effective teachers engage in deliberate decision making, resulting from the specific ways they think about teaching and learning.

Highly effective teachers engage in deliberate decision making, resulting from the specific ways they think about teaching and learning (see Figure 1.3).

Figure 1.3 What makes an effective teacher?

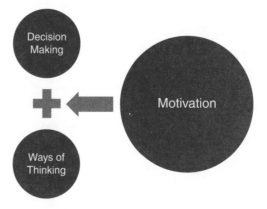

This decision making and ways of thinking are fueled by teachers' motivation for student growth and achievement.

Teacher Decision Making

If great teaching requires great decision making, what goes into a teacher like Mr. Booth's decision making? Understanding the decision-making process has long been an interest to researchers (e.g., Kahneman & Tversky, 2000). According to those who study decision making in human beings, this process includes: (1) recognizing that a decision is necessary, (2) gathering evidence to weigh and consider options, (3) taking action on one or more of those options, and (4) reviewing the impact of the decision.

Mr. Booth's internal dialogue leads him to make the decisions based on several steps. "First, I recognize that it is really up to me to make the right decisions about what happens in my classroom. After all, I am the teacher." This kind of comment shows that good ideas can stop at the classroom door, or at logging into the remote environment, unless the teacher has intentions and plans to implement these ideas. Teachers are great filters (of good and bad ideas). Also, we cannot overstate the importance of the relationship between Mr. Booth's teaching and his students' learning. He recognizes the power in his decisions and the influence this has on the learning outcomes of his students. If you take two students, comparing them side-by-side, it matters less which school they attend and more on the teacher in the classroom (Hattie & Zierer, 2019).

Recognizing that there is value, potential, and therefore power in our decisions, the next step in the decision-making process is the gathering of information. "This is where I spend most of my time. I have to not only know what I want students to learn, but I have to know what they already know. I have to get them to show me what they come through the door already knowing about motion, forces, electricity, or whatever we are learning that day." As educators gather information, or evidence, about students' prior knowledge or background knowledge, they can identify the possible pathways or routes through learning progressions. Teachers must weigh the evidence carefully to consider all of the possible options for moving learning forward, and then they must choose the options they believe are best in light of that evidence.

Mr. Booth points out, "After I have a plan on what to do in class, the fun part is setting it up. If I decide to use a jigsaw, I have to plan the selections and groups. If I decide to do a lab, I have to set it up." Making a decision about how to move learning forward leads directly to taking action. However, taking action must be accompanied by a means for later reviewing that decision. "As I start setting things up, I begin to think about how I am going to check in on my students to make sure they are with me. I mean, if we are going to do a jigsaw or complete a lab, I have to make sure they actually learned something. Looking through a microscope at cells is fun, but I have to ask myself, did it do anything for them?"

As we noted in the Introduction, highly effective teachers have the ability to make the right decisions, at the right time, for the right experience with their learners. When done well, teachers' decision-making processes are the result of a deliberate internal dialogue that presents as high impact teaching and learning. Internal dialogue and the subsequent decisions are part of a larger way of thinking. John Hattie calls them *mindframes* (Hattie & Zierer, 2018).

Ways of Thinking and Decision Making

"How we think about the impact of what we do is more important than what we do" (Hattie & Zierer, 2018, p. ix). This thinking is evident in educator's decision making, and not just in their second-by-second decision making. Specific mindframes drive ways of thinking, ways of supporting our colleagues and students, and the enthusiasm and passion individuals have for teaching and learning. Mr. Booth's mindframes around his role as a middle school science teacher move well beyond a singular set of decisions around microscopes, cells, and entrance tickets. It really is all about how Mr. Booth and the rest of us think about the work we do in our learning environments. There is empirical evidence that correlates the decision making of teachers with their mindframes (Hattie & Zierer, 2018).

There are 10 mindframes that manifest themselves in the decisions that teachers make. These mindframes have a pronounced impact on how teachers teach and students learn. The first three mindframes relate to how educators think about their impact on student learning:

1. I am an evaluator of my impact on student learning.

2. I see assessment as informing my impact and next steps.

3. I collaborate with my peers and my students about conceptions of progress and my impact.

Let's step away from Mr. Booth's classroom for a moment and visit Katy Campbell's fourth-grade class. She is planning for her upcoming literacy block and has started by reviewing her learners' responses to an online reading comprehension task from the previous day. "I always spend time looking at their work from the day before. Their responses, whether it is what I am looking for or not, let me see how I am doing in my own teaching." Ms. Campbell then uses this information to decide where to go next with her learners. In her words, "This is important for me in deciding where to go next with them and what strategies or interventions I might use to move their learning forward. In some cases, I set up remote conferences with them to plan the next steps based on their own individual reading goals."

Ms. Campbell clearly sees herself as an evaluator of her own impact on student learning. She uses this information to inform the next steps in her teaching and their learning and not simply for a grade. Her mindframes around her impact on student learning directly inform her decision making. As part of her own decision making, Ms. Campbell regularly asks herself how she knows her teaching is working, how one approach compares with another, what is the merit of her using one particular approach over another, and what evidence she needs to evaluate the impact of her teaching on her students' learning. "At first, this was a challenge using remote learning. However, I soon realized that there are tools out there that allow me to see how they are progressing in their learning."

The next two mindframes relate to how educators think about change and challenge in their face-to-face classrooms or remote learning environments.

1. I am a change agent and believe all students can improve.

2. I strive for challenge and not merely "doing your best."

For example, who is the change agent in your learning environment? While primarily the teacher can be, this does not imply that learners are not involved in the learning process. Instead, these mindframes acknowledge that we, as teachers, have the potential to have the greatest impact on student learning. To do this, we must accept the challenge and prepare learners to engage in the challenge of learning. The art of teaching is knowing what is appropriately challenging for one child and what level of challenge is appropriate for another.

We must see ourselves as change agents who embrace challenges in the learning process. For example, let's look into the thinking of another teacher, high school physics teacher Thomas O'Neill. He approaches his role from a change-agent mindframe. "For my students, they walk into this class with prior experiences and conceptions about how the world works. I take it as my personal responsibility to ensure that my teaching engages them in a way that prompts conceptual change." Mr. O'Neill recognizes that the ways in which he plans, designs, and implements his instruction can serve as the activator for student learning. In science, this is referred to as conceptual change, but this idea is generalizable across all disciplines.

Learning is hard and takes time. This does not stop Mr. O'Neill from embracing that challenge and then supporting his students as they wrestle with the difficulty and complexity of knowledge and skills demanded in his discipline. In English language arts there is a process of editing and revising, in mathematics we must verify our solutions and approach to problem solving, in social studies we have to triangulate data to support our historical inferences, and, finally, in science, there is the nature of science and refuting hypotheses. Regardless of the discipline or content area, educators and their students must recognize that the learning will be, and should be, challenging.

But, we also have to support our learners in their approach and progress through these challenges. Do we help learners see the value of concentration, persistence, and deliberate practice? "I do not take the standpoint that physics is hard, but that the learning experience should challenge learners thinking. I have to get them to lean into that challenge. This compels me to look at learners as individuals and then support each one as they engage in the learning. At the end of the day, they have to feel supported and secure in my class if I am going to expect them to take a risk and dive into a challenging problem, scenario, or task."

This last comment by Mr. O'Neill leads directly to the remaining five mindframes, which focus on learning. How do we talk about our role as a teacher?

1. I give and help students understand feedback, and I interpret and act on feedback given to me.

2. I engage as much in dialogue as monologue.

3. I explicitly inform students what successful impact looks like from the outset.

4. I build relationships and trust so that learning can occur in a place where it is safe to make mistakes and learn from others.

5. I focus on learning and the language of learning.

Specifically, do we reference our teaching or our students' learning? These five mindframes place student learning at the forefront of decision making and our work. Now, to be clear, the implication is not that teaching does not matter—teaching matters a lot. However, one separator between those who have a high impact on student learning and those that do not (yet), is the focus on learning rather than teaching.

Let's explore this idea and these five mindframes a bit more. Here is a nonexample. In the teacher's workroom, a conversation was overheard between two mathematics teachers. "Well, I taught them congruent triangles and gave them a lot of opportunities to practice. I even explained to them how they could remember the relationships: S-S-S, S-A-S, A-A-S, A-S-A." This comment was followed by a response, "I don't know what else we can do." When we look at this brief exchange, let's first acknowledge that we have all been in this position. And, naturally, we can easily slip into a list of things we did. However, a different way of thinking is required if we want to have an impact. Consider this alternative: "I need to better understand my students' learning by getting them to dialogue with me. What are their ideas, questions, struggles, and views about this content?" What are they stuck on, what do they not know that would then help them understand? This includes, but is not limited to, engaging in dialogue with learners; seeking their feedback, including expectations for success; and acknowledging the role of mistakes as opportunities to learn.

These 10 mindframes drive the teacher's decision making about teaching. These mindframes influence the decisions teachers make, including the daily choices made during a literacy block or in afternoon geometry class. So, what is the root of these mindframes and how can we nurture them in all of us and our colleagues? As you might suspect, the fuel that drives this process is motivation.

Motivation and Decision Making

Think back to when you were a student in school. Remember the common question you were asked: What do you want to be when you grow up? If you answered teacher, what were the reasons? And, have those reasons changed since you made the decision to enter the field? One of the authors of this book, John Almarode, knew he wanted to be a teacher from the time he stepped out of his kindergarten year. Over the years, he became more focused on becoming a science teacher and then a teacher educator. His initial motivation to teach was sparked in elementary school by his own teachers. It was then Ms. Cross, his sixth-grade science teacher, who really fanned the flame. All of this occurred early in his education. On the other hand, it is possible that some of us entered the profession as a second or third career move. For those of us in that situation, the reasons for becoming a teacher may differ. The truth is, some of us did not plan to be a teacher when we were children. For example, Vince did not decide to go into teaching until a professor at his university suggested he try it as a career option. Although he had to change his major, he decided to pursue teaching and has not looked back since. Nancy started teaching her stuffed animals long before setting up classes for her neighbors and then earning her credentials. One of the commonalities amongst these stories is the modeling or, or at the very least, goading of someone already in the profession. For them, teaching was a passion and it was contagious. Like Mr. Booth, Ms. Cross, or Vince's university professor, teaching is less of a career and more of a lifestyle they have embraced as their identity.

This passion, lifestyle, and identity are not shared by everyone. You likely have heard the saying: *those who can't do, teach*? Yes, the hair on the back of our necks stands up no matter how many times we hear that statement. Although this may change in the future, the reality is that we are living in a time when education struggles for legitimacy in the eyes of the public. There are many reasons for this disconnect between our view of teaching and learning and the public's view of what goes on in our schools. One possible reason might be the fact that nearly every member of the public went to school and has occupied the role of a student. Given that they have been students at some point in their lives, they have years of experience in schools. These experiences lead to the strongly held belief that what worked for them in school should work for everyone. After all, "that is what we had to do when I was in school."

The relationship between motivation and decision making to become a teacher often plays out in front of our eyes. For all of us, the initial understanding of teaching and learning came from our direct experiences as students and learners in the many classrooms we occupied while growing up. As teachers, the experiences we had in school play a direct role in how we see ourselves as teachers. For example, what motivated Mr. Booth to become a teacher was another teacher. Thus, Mr. Booth's model for what goes into teaching and learning is derived from that influential individual. Likewise, John Almarode's classroom is modeled after Ms. Cross's sixth-grade science classroom. The imitation of our favorite or most influential teacher will likely limit our impact on student learning. Although an essential part of each teacher's professional and personal story, this approach replicates what our most influential teachers did, but not the thinking that led to the doing. The message we hope to convey in this book is that the thinking behind our teaching best drives our decision making.

There are other motivating factors that need to be considered and, in most every situation, influence our decision making. Understanding what encompasses teacher motivation can, in turn, guide us to keep the very best of us in the field and can create the potential for long-lasting, high-quality teaching.

Teacher Motivation

When looking at what motivates someone to become a teacher, the general public tends to think of extrinsic motivations that drive people to pursue education as a career (e.g., stable job, decent wage, summers off, or great holidays). These tend to be the reasons for the discontent toward the education system from certain sectors of the public. The misunderstanding and lack of clarity between what people think teachers do and what teachers actually do can lead to misconceptions surrounding why teachers decide to enter this field. Watt and Richardson (2007) examined the concept of teacher motivation across multiple contexts. While both authors are based out of Australia, the creation of the FIT-Choice (Factors Influencing Teacher Choice) framework has been used to examine teacher motivation across the world (see Figure 1.4). The FIT-Choice model was developed "to assess the primary motivations of teachers to teach" (Watt, Richardson, & Smith, 2017, p. 6). This model was created to standardize the research on motivation that, in the past, relied on locally created questionnaires and scales. In other words, we did not have an agreed-upon method to study why some individuals chose teaching as a profession, while others did not. This created a problem in that we could not compare, synthesize, or generalize findings on teacher motivation. Understanding teacher motivation is important: Just as our own awareness about what motivates learners (e.g., autonomy, efficacy, connectedness, etc.) helps us design and implement experiences that enhance their learning, if we have a better idea about motivation there is a greater chance that we can do the same for future and current teachers.

The FIT-Choice model has been applied around the globe as a means to provide a common language around what motivates individuals to enter into the teaching profession.

When looking at the key elements of the model (i.e., socialization and intrinsic value), the framework assesses factors that can encourage or discourage teachers from entering teaching. It is

Figure 1.4 A way to understanding teacher motivation

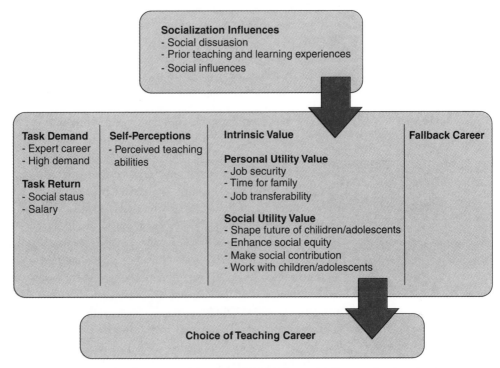

Socialization Influences
- Social dissuasion
- Prior teaching and learning experiences
- Social influences

Task Demand
- Expert career
- High demand

Task Return
- Social staus
- Salary

Self-Perceptions
- Perceived teaching abilities

Intrinsic Value

Personal Utility Value
- Job security
- Time for family
- Job transferability

Social Utility Value
- Shape future of chilidren/adolescents
- Enhance social equity
- Make social contribution
- Work with children/adolescents

Fallback Career

Choice of Teaching Career

Source: Watt, H. M. G., Richardson, P. W., & Smith, K. (2017). Why teach? How teachers' motivations matter around the world. In H. M. G. Watt, P. W. Richardson & K. Smith (Eds.), *Global perspectives on teacher motivation* (p. 1 - 21). Cambridge: Cambridge University Press.

through this model that Watt et al. (2017) engaged in a global analysis of teacher motivations. Let's unpack the model here and look at how this shapes our ultimate decision making.

For Vince and John Almarode, their initial influence came from socialization—their prior teaching and learning experiences as well as the influence of a university professor and sixth-grade science teacher. From there, Watt et al. (2017) found that "people who choose teaching as a career are motivated by a complex interaction of factors embedded within communities and cultural expectations but seem generally to embrace a desire to undertake meaningful work that makes for a better, more equitable society" (p. 5). This may be surprising to some of you reading this book, especially considering that teachers are often accused of entering the profession for extrinsic reasons (e.g., "summers off"). That's right, teachers like Mr. Vasquez, Ms. Meyer, Mr. Booth, and Ms. Cross were most likely motivated to enter the teaching profession because of intrinsic and altruistic reasons. In Figure 1.4, we see this under the category of Social Utility Value. For Mr. Booth specifically, he feels a sense of personal responsibility to engage with middle school students in a positive and supportive way. In the end, this will make a social contribution to the community and, if done well, enhance social equity. Many teachers feel personally responsible for the success of their students, as well as the level of teaching that they are providing them. If you need direct and tangible evidence of this motivation, ask yourself this question: how much of your own money do you spend on your students and supplies every year? Or, if not money, how many hours outside of the traditional school day do you spend on planning, instruction, and assessment?

These actions are not unique. As a matter of fact, they are more commonplace than not, and much of this has to do with the intrinsic motivations that drive teachers to feel personally responsible for their students (often referred to as "my kids"). This notion is supported by the work of Lauermann, Karabenick, Carpenter, and Kuusinen (2017), who used the FIT-Choice framework in their analysis of teacher motivation and teacher efficacy. In their study they "confirmed positive relations between intrinsic and social motivations for teaching" and "all three indicators of professional commitment (personal time investment, interest in professional development and commitment to teaching as a career)" (p. 335). Butler (2017) highlighted the following conclusion after examining teacher motivations across the globe:

> On average, teachers from different social backgrounds in different countries and educational settings perceive teaching in rather similar ways and choose to teach for very similar and, in motivational terms, very positive kinds of reasons. (p. 379)

Most enter teaching because they can have an impact on students.

Motivation and Implementation

Leslie Blair, a veteran teacher of over 20 years, describes teaching as the best thing that has ever happened to her. She can often be overheard talking about the students as her own children alongside remarks that being a teacher has never felt like hard work because she loves being in the classroom with her students. This pure joy that Ms. Blair has for her students has made her one of the favorites around Riverside Middle School, and it is not just because she is always smiling. Ms. Blair actively seeks out strategies and resources that provide ways to improve her craft. She can be found reading professional learning books, attending professional development workshops, and often talking to younger teachers about their teaching strategies. Ms. Blair is a consummate professional. She is often tapped by her administration team to lead staff through professional development based on the strategies she has been learning and applying in her practice. Ms. Blair loves to share her knowledge and her thinking with all staff and proves time and time again that age and experience are not a reason to stop learning and evaluating your practice. When asked why she doesn't intend to slow down, her answer is always the same, "To be the best teacher for my students, I need to be a student myself!"

Down the hallway, Mr. Sharp is currently in his fourth-year teaching, his first at Riverside Middle. He is a hardworking, passionate teacher who loves his students but often considers leaving the profession. When you spend a day in Mr. Sharp's classroom, you can tell he is a teacher who loves being with his students. His lessons are often engaging, and very much aligned with the curriculum. His students love having him as their teacher; he is kind, smart, and willing to interact with students on multiple levels. He listens, he cares, he teaches. They often remark about how relatable he is to them as individuals and learners. Although engaging and relatable to students, Mr. Sharp is considering leaving the profession to pursue other career opportunities. When talking about the consideration to leave, Mr. Sharp talks about loving being around students but does not love all the other aspects that accompany teaching (meetings, professional development, marking, and planning). He acknowledges that he does not enjoy engaging in professional development as he does not see the point of learning more. He views his current practice as good enough for students and remarks they are learning. It is worth noting that he continues to apply the same strategies he applied in his first year. He mentions that during his first year, he applied all he learned in his pre-service program and tied everything back to the curriculum. He even mentions that his teaching works, so why try something new that might backfire. Mr. Sharp is doing enough to get by and does not have the desire to learn something new or to continue in the profession.

Based on their decision making and thinking, one of these teachers at Riverside Middle could be classified as expert (Ms. Blair) and the other as a novice (Mr. Sharp). Again, this is based on their thinking about their teaching and not for the seniority they hold. A common misconception is that expert teachers are the most veteran in the room. This is not always true as on many occasions we can find veterans who have adopted the "if it ain't broke, don't fix it" mentality which can manifest itself in stagnant teaching practice and the lessening of their impact on student learning. They can become reluctant learners to improve the impact of their teaching. We are not saying that all teachers who hold seniority have that mentality; we just want to make it clear that experience does not equal expertise. In the case of Ms. Blair, she is of both categories, expert and experienced. The reason being is that she has made deliberate choices to evaluate her impact and to stay current with valuable teaching strategies that positively impact her students in her classroom. This is the result of how she thinks about her role as a teacher, driven by her motivation to enter the profession. So, what do we do to influence the beliefs, or ways of thinking, and increase the motivation for teaching and learning?

A Shared Language for Great Teaching

That we can find two teachers who work in the same school, teaching the same subject, and yet have very different motivations when it comes to teaching is amazing. We can assume that there is more intrinsic motivation with Ms. Blair as it seems she has fully committed herself to being the best possible teacher for her students. It is also important to note that while Mr. Sharp is intending on leaving the profession, he is a well-respected teacher in the school and the students love him. What is important to notice about Ms. Blair and Mr. Sharp is the notion that our motivations can deeply impact our thinking, which, in turn, impacts our decision making. However, we need every teacher in the building to maximize his or her impact on every student in the building. Therefore, we cannot focus on Ms. Blair and wish Mr. Sharp the best in his next career. On the other hand, we cannot ignore Ms. Blair and overwhelm Mr. Sharp with instructional coaching, professional development, and endless plans of improvement. We need to find ways of making the difference together. The greatest impact on student learning comes from leveraging the individual efficacy, or expectations of success, into a collective whole. This approach not only recognizes that together we have a greater impact on student learning, but also recognizes that we must work to foster and nurture that collective effort.

Collective teacher efficacy is the belief of a teacher group in the collective ability to promote student success in their school. With an average effect size of 1.39 (Hattie & Zierer, 2019), this particular influence carries a greater potential in accelerating the learning in our schools than having clear learning intentions, student engagement, formative evaluation, and feedback. The effect size for collective teacher efficacy is greater than the effect size for socioeconomic status, immigrant status, and gender. Although each of these influences is important and cannot be ignored, the very idea that the collective beliefs teachers have such incredible potential means that we can, if you will allow the use of this phrase, "leave no teacher behind" in our efforts to engage in better teaching by design. To be blunt, we need Ms. Blair and Mr. Sharp to be great teachers, not by chance, but by design. We need Mr. Booth, Ms. Campbell, Mr. O'Neill, and all of our colleagues to engage in great teaching, by design.

To achieve this collective goal, we have to ensure that each of these teachers, as well as our colleagues and ourselves, have a shared language of teaching and learning. If we are to affect the motivation of colleagues that see their role differently from Ms. Blair, we must have a shared language of learning so that we can communicate about our thinking. If we are to affect the thinking of colleagues that do not have the mindframes associated with greater impact, we need a shared language of learning so that we can talk about decision making. And finally, if we are to channel our knowledge about what works best in teaching and learning into effective implementation, actualized potential, and informed decisions, we have to have a shared language for implementation. That is exactly what the DIIE model sets out to do!

Now, let's get started with an in-depth look at each component of the model and how we *implement and evaluate what works best.*

"

We must discover where our learners are in their learning relative to where we aim for them to be at the end of a particular learning experience.

2

CHAPTER 2

DIAGNOSIS AND DISCOVERY

Figure 2.1   The DIIE model

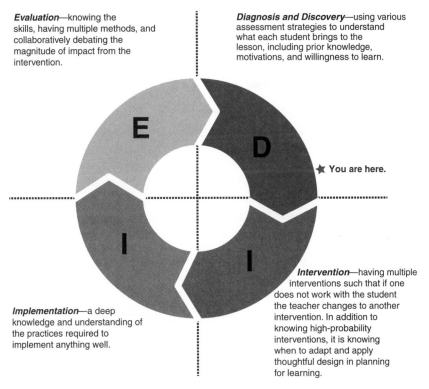

Evaluation—knowing the skills, having multiple methods, and collaboratively debating the magnitude of impact from the intervention.

Diagnosis and Discovery—using various assessment strategies to understand what each student brings to the lesson, including prior knowledge, motivations, and willingness to learn.

★ You are here.

Intervention—having multiple interventions such that if one does not work with the student the teacher changes to another intervention. In addition to knowing high-probability interventions, it is knowing when to adapt and apply thoughtful design in planning for learning.

Implementation—a deep knowledge and understanding of the practices required to implement anything well.

Knowing what intervention or approach will most likely ensure learning requires that teachers have a robust understanding of where each of their learners is in their learning journey. Furthermore, knowing what alterations to make to an intervention or approach requires an understanding of the local context, including the dispositions, unique characteristics, and learning experiences learners bring to the learning environment. This necessitates a diagnosis. The main idea for this chapter, then, is that success in moving from intention to implementation, and subsequently having an impact on our students' learning, requires that teachers know their learners and where they are in the learning journey.

As we eavesdrop on Diane Henry's mathematics block, we get a glimpse of this component of the DIIE model in action. "Before I begin a new topic or unit in mathematics, I give my second graders a problem related to the new learning. Today, two-digit subtraction, with re-grouping." The buzz in the room is noticeable. Ms. Henry's second graders are busy working through a scenario that pre-assesses their background or prior knowledge in both regrouping and subtraction. As her learners engage in the scenario, she observes their dialogue, behaviors, and their interactions with their peers.

"I am not just observing their understanding of place-value and subtraction, although that is very important. I am listening to their use of mathematics language, their choice of problem-solving methods and manipulatives, and, then, also, how they engage in a challenging task with their peers. Are they motivated to engage in tough problems? Can they work cooperatively in these tough situations?" Ms. Henry is not only considering her students' content knowledge. She is also examining their current dispositions, unique characteristics, and learning experiences in behavioral and social-emotional areas.

When selecting the best interventions for the current content or skills, we do not start with the just the *what* (i.e., place-value, two-digit subtraction, regrouping, etc.). We also need to know the *who* (i.e., dispositions, unique characteristics, and learning opportunities). This requires that we take an in-depth look at what is meant by *diagnose* in the DIIE model, which we are just about ready to do. However, before that, we want to provide some clarification on the terminology.

Many of us recoil a bit at the use of the word *diagnose*. In our initial exploration of this model, we did the same thing. The word *diagnose* has negative connotations of disease and ailments based on symptoms of some underlying pathology. This is unfortunate. When we consider the origin and meaning of the word *diagnose*, we find a much more robust meaning that makes the term *diagnose* exactly the right term for the message we need to guide our decision making in the learning environment. Several of us (the authors) enjoy studying word origins and, in this case, looking into the origins of this word provides a better context for our discussion.

The origin of the word *diagnose* can be traced back to the combination of the Greek stem, *dia*, with *gignoskein*. *Dia* is a stem that means "between" and *gignoskein* means "to learn" or "come to know." When we put these two parts together, we arrive at the Greek word *diagignoskein*, and from there, the word, *diagnosis*. When we focus on the root meaning of the word *diagnosis*, this brings us to a

---

When selecting the best interventions for the current content or skills, we do not start with the just the *what* (i.e., place-value, two-digit subtraction, regrouping, etc.). We also need to know the *who* (i.e., dispositions, unique characteristics, and learning opportunities).

more robust definition of, a discerning, distinguishing, or to come to know thoroughly or apart (Beekes, 2010). This is exactly what we mean when we use the word *diagnose* in the DIIE model. There is nothing pathological or related to the identification of a disease or ailment in our learners. Instead, the first component in the DIIE model requires that we thoroughly know our learners and seek to discern where they are in their learning—academic, behavioral, and social-emotional. As shown in Figure 2.2, we must discover where they are in their learning relative to where we aim for them to be at

We must discover where our learners are in their learning relative to where we aim for them to be at the end of a particular learning experience.

Figure 2.2 Diagnosing and discovering the gap

Where are my learners now?

Where are we going?

Photo by Sammie Vasquez on Unsplash

the end of a particular learning experience. Closing this gap is our primary objective as teachers.

The Who Behind the Learning

A key element of discerning where our learners are, is to also determine the context in which our students are learning. To determine context, teachers should also be asking, *who is learning with me?* (Bustamante & Almarode, 2020). Through this question, we should devote time to thinking about the environment in which students are conducting learning both at school and at home. This includes the physical, social, and emotional environment. Will they have a place to focus on their learning? Who else is in their environment with them? Are they, themselves anxious, uncertain, or ill? The answers to each of these questions introduce additional variables into the learning equation—variables that absolutely cannot be ignored for the sake of multiplying fractions, learning about cellular reproduction, understanding the author's purpose, and analyzing historical documents. The *who* behind the *do* is immeasurably important. Ensuring that we have clarity about *who* is learning will ultimately determine the impact we will be able to *do* with and for our learners.

Using various assessment strategies to understand what each student brings to the lesson—including their prior knowledge, motivations, and willingness to learn—allows teachers to make effective and efficient decisions about where to go next in the learning.

In other words, how far apart are the learning expectations from the current dispositions, unique characteristics, and learning opportunities of our learners? The intervention and implementation must close this gap between what students know and can do, and what they need to know and be able to do. Using various assessment strategies to understand what each student brings to the lesson—including their prior knowledge, motivations, and willingness to learn—allows teachers to make effective and efficient decisions about where to go next in the learning.

Here is our path forward through this component of the model. To diagnose and discover the current dispositions, unique characteristics, and learning opportunities of our learners, we must:

1. Analyze the learning expectations (e.g., national or local standards) to understand what learners must know, understand, and be able to do in a given grade or content area.

2. Design and implement initial assessments that diagnose and discover gaps in student knowledge, skills, and understandings.

3. Use expert teacher-noticing to attend to student responses surrounding those initial assessments and make sense of that information (see Figure 2.3).

Figure 2.3 The essential parts of diagnosing or discovering

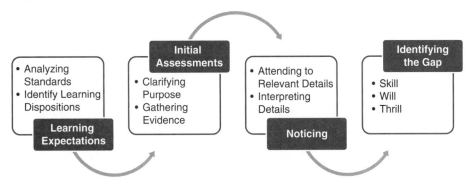

Standards of and for Learning as the Starting Point

For most of us, where we are going in our teaching and learning is driven by standards of learning. Whether your standards are national expectations or specific to a state or province, these official documents set the expectations for learners in that particular year of schooling. For example, in the United States, states adopt standards for each subject area. In Canada, the standards are unique to each province while Australia and New Zealand have national standards. Although standards vary depending on where we teach, all of us must start with analyzing the standards to identify the concepts and skills within each one. Let's return to Ms. Henry's classroom and understand the process she engaged in to develop a clear picture of where her learners were going.

In Grade 2 mathematics, Ms. Henry engages in the DIIE model by first looking at the mathematics standards for this unit on sums and differences.

The student will

a) estimate sums and differences;

b) determine sums and differences, using various methods; and

c) create and solve single-step and two-step practical problems involving addition and subtraction.

Source: Virginia Department of Education. (2016). *Mathematics standards of learning*. Virginia Department of Education: Richmond, VA.

In addition to the core standard for this unit, Ms. Henry must spend time analyzing the curriculum framework and other supporting documents that accompany the core standard. For this specific standard, there are essential skills and knowledge articulated by the state's Department of Education.

The student will use problem solving, mathematical communication, mathematical reasoning, connections, and representations to

- Estimate the sum of two whole numbers whose sum is 99 or less and recognize whether the estimation is reasonable (e.g., 27 + 41 is about 70, because 27 is about 30 and 41 is about 40, and 30 + 40 is 70). Refers to (a) in the standard.

- Estimate the difference between two whole numbers each 99 or less and recognize whether the estimate is reasonable. Refers to (a) in the standard.

- Determine the sum of two whole numbers whose sum is 99 or less, using various methods. Refers to (b) in the standard.

- Determine the difference of two whole numbers each 99 or less, using various methods. Refers to (b) in the standard.

- Create and solve single-step practical problems involving addition or subtraction. Refers to (c) in the standard.

- Create and solve two-step practical problems involving addition, subtraction, or both addition and subtraction. Refers to (c) in the standard.

Source: Virginia Department of Education. (2016). *Mathematics standards of learning*. Virginia Department of Education: Richmond, VA.

Ms. Henry's grade-level team starts by identifying the concepts contained within this standard and supporting documents. These concepts, often identified as the nouns or noun phrases, provide a picture of what knowledge, ideas, and terms learners will be expected to master (see Tables 2.1, 2.2, and 2.3 for examples). In addition, they must determine what skills are expected in this learning by identifying the verbs or verb phrases within the standard. What will their learners be expected to do as a result of their learning? This should include processes or practices associated with a particular discipline (e.g., science and engineering practices, social studies and literacy skills, and college/career readiness skills).

At the end of this analysis, Ms. Henry and her colleagues have a clear picture of the expectations for their learners. They have an understanding of what learners are expected to know, understand, and be able to do within the context of sums and differences. But there is one final aspect of this process that takes into account the dispositions of learners.

Table 2.1 Analyzing the standard for concepts and skills

Concepts (Nouns)	Skills (Verbs)	Mathematical Practices
sums	estimate	problem solving
differences	determine	reasoning
methods (approaches)	create	communicating
whole numbers	solve	connecting
estimation (reasonable)		representing (modeling)
addition		
subtraction		
practical		

At William Perry Primary School, the faculty spent time over the past summer to develop dispositional expectations of a learner. In other words, the entire school has embraced a common definition of what it means to be a "good learner" at William Perry. These dispositional traits include cooperation, perseverance, and respect. Therefore, Ms. Henry and her colleagues must analyze where these fit into this unit and where they expect their second graders to be in each of these areas. Furthermore, these dispositional traits transcend the physical learning environment. They can and should be a part of a remote learning environment as well. What are the expectations for collaborative learning with peers, strategies for persevering, and demonstrating respect for all members of the school and learning community?

Before moving on, let's look briefly at two other examples from Canada and England.

General Outcome

Students will explore the impacts of globalization on their lives.

Specific Outcomes

Values and Attitudes

Students will:

1.1 acknowledge and appreciate the existence of multiple perspectives in a globalizing world.

1.2 appreciate why peoples in Canada and other locations strive to promote their cultures, languages, and identities in a globalizing world.

(Continued)

(Continued)

1.3 appreciate how identities and cultures shape, and are shaped by, globalization.

Knowledge and Understanding

Students will:

1.4 explore ways in which individuals and collectives express identities (traditions, language, religion, spirituality, the arts, attire, relationship to land, ideological beliefs, role modeling).

Source: Alberta Learning. (2007). *Social Studies 10-1* [Program of Studies]. Edmonton, Canada: Alberta Learning.

Table 2.2   Analyzing the standard for concepts and skills

Concepts (Nouns)	Skills (Verbs)	Dimensions of Thinking
globalization	explore	critical thinking
culture	acknowledge	creative thinking
language	appreciate	historical thinking
identities		geographic thinking
traditions		
religion		
spirituality		
arts		
attire		
relationship to land		
ideological beliefs		
role modeling		

Stage 4 Reading

Pupils should be taught to

- read and appreciate the depth and power of the English literary heritage through

  o reading a wide range of high-quality, challenging, classic literature and extended literary nonfiction, such as essays, reviews, and journalism. This writing should include whole texts. The range will include:

    - at least one play by Shakespeare

    - works from the 19th, 20th, and 21st centuries

    - poetry since 1789, including representative Romantic poetry

- o re-reading literature and other writing as a basis for making comparisons
- o choosing and reading books independently for challenge, interest, and enjoyment
- understand and critically evaluate texts through
  - o reading in different ways for different purposes, summarising and synthesising ideas and information, and evaluating their usefulness for particular purposes
  - o drawing on knowledge of the purpose, audience for, and context of the writing, including its social, historical, and cultural context and the literary tradition to which it belongs, to inform evaluation
  - o identifying and interpreting themes, ideas, and information
  - o exploring aspects of plot, characterisation, events, and settings, the relationships between them and their effects
  - o seeking evidence in the text to support a point of view, including justifying inferences with evidence
  - o distinguishing between statements that are supported by evidence and those that are not, and identifying bias and misuse of evidence
  - o analysing a writer's choice of vocabulary, form, grammatical and structural features, and evaluating their effectiveness and impact
  - o making critical comparisons, referring to the contexts, themes, characterisation, style, and literary quality of texts, and drawing on knowledge and skills from wider reading
- make an informed personal response, recognizing that other responses to a text are possible and evaluating these.

Source: Department for Education. (2014) The national curriculum in England: Complete framework for key stages 1 to 4. Available at: https://www.gov.uk/government/publications/national-curriculum-in-england-framework-for-key-stages-1-to-4 (Accessed July, 21, 2020).

Table 2.3 Analyzing the standard for concepts and skills

Concepts (Nouns)	Skills (Verbs)	Literacy Skills
literary heritage	summarising	inferring
context (social, historical, cultural)	synthesising	referring to evidence in text

(Continued)

Table 2.3 (Continued)

Concepts (Nouns)	Skills (Verbs)	Literacy Skills
literary tradition	identifying	knowing purpose
themes	interpreting	comprehension
plots	exploring	reading critically
characterisation	seeking (evidence)	vocabulary building
features (grammatical and structural)	distinguishing	
literary quality	analysing	
Shakespeare	making comparisons	
literary time periods		

Note: British spellings are used in Table 2.3, reflecting the standard from the national curriculum in England.

In the end, these teachers have defined the right side of the cliff in Figure 2.2. They now know where their learners are going. But, the whole idea behind diagnosis or discovery is to discern where students are in their learning relative to where we aim for them to be at the end of a particular learning experience. To do this, we must analyze standards and design initial assessments that accomplish two goals:

1. What do the learners already know, understand, and are able to do related to the specific concepts, skills, practices, and dispositions in this standard?

2. What relevant prior learning have the learners retained and are able to retrieve (e.g., whole numbers, estimation, and communication)?

The analysis of standards and knowing where we are going sets the stage for us to look backwards and forward in diagnosing where students are in their learning.

Initial Assessments

When we engage in discovering what our students bring to the learning environment and each individual learning experience or engaging task, we must take into account students' background knowledge, prior knowledge, skills, and understandings. Ms. Clouse, an English teacher in the Midwest, shares that, "I cannot move forward with any learning until I have a clear picture of where my learners are in their own learning. For English 10, I need to not only have a grasp of what they know about the content, but I need to make sure I know their skill level in reading and writing as well. They can talk to me all day about the definitions, but if there is a gap with their reading comprehension skills and writing skills, that may stop us from actualizing their potential. I am always afraid that I will miss a learning opportunity that will hinder later progress." What Ms. Clouse is talking about is the evidence provided by incorporating pre- or initial assessments into our diagnosis and discovery of our learners. Some estimates are that learners already know about 60 percent of what we expect them to learn (Nuthall, 2007). The initial assessment can be of great value to teachers, in both time and understanding of students' knowledge.

The purpose of the initial assessment is for us to gather evidence about students and their background knowledge and prior knowledge. Hockett and Doubet (2014) explain the initial assessment as "a way to gather evidence of students' readiness, interests, or learning profiles before beginning a lesson or unit and then using that evidence to plan instruction that will meet learners' needs" (p. 50). This strategy essentially serves to inform us about "where the student is" in their journey, and this information can inform next steps for learning. This evidence also serves as a reminder of what we may not have to explicitly teach simply because our learners are already proficient in the content or skills. To be clear, this does not mean that we do not have to use checks for understanding and progress monitoring to ensure retention. Ms. Clouse recalls a situation where she felt like valuable instructional time was wasted because she did not initially assess her learners. "Imagine coming into a unit on figurative language, devoting an entire week to the different types of figurative language only to find out that their success in this particular content and its application comes from the fact that they already knew about similes, metaphors, hyperbole, personifications, etc. . . . To add to this, because I did not initially assess my learners about symbolic representation, our literary analysis of *Lord of the Flies* by William Golding proved to be difficult and challenging for reasons above and beyond the learning intentions and success criteria. I had no idea what tripped them up because I did not ask."

> The purpose of the initial assessment is for us to gather evidence about students and their background knowledge and prior knowledge.

Initial assessments prior to teaching new content or skills help us diagnose and discover what learners already know and can do. This allows us to make better decisions about where to go next in the learning journey. Guskey and McTighe (2016) discuss the importance of taking into account the prior knowledge students bring to any learning situation, as paramount to the learning of new information. They note that "if new learning is built on a base of previous knowledge, it stands to reason that teachers should find out what students know, or think they know about new topics or concepts" (p. 39).

Table 2.4 Examples of different ways to determine what students know and don't know yet

entrance tickets
think-pair-shares
writing prompts
anchor problems
reading responses
mini-laboratory
open-ended questions
class discussion
student-generated questions
concept or thinking map

An initial assessment should not be considered a "pre-test." This is often an error in understanding that leads to a misuse of the initial assessment as a high-influence strategy and limits the value of the evidence generated by the assessment. A main reason to differentiate between an initial assessment and a pre-test has to do with the purpose of the assessment. An initial assessment is used to determine what our students know and do not know, yet, also necessary for us to make decisions about the implementation of specific interventions that will move students closer to where we are going in the learning. Table 2.4 illustrates some different types of initial assessments.

While a pre-test is often followed up with a post-test at the end of the unit and provides us data for calculating growth, this testing scenario can cause some complications for the discovery process, especially when these evaluations are linked to grades. One fast and furious way to disrupt an environment that encourages mistakes and errors, put a grade on it. Guskey (2018) highlighted the potential complications of pre- and post-testing as follows, "When teachers base students' grades on progress from pre-test to post-test, students recognize that doing poorly on the pre-test enhances their chances to show improvement and earn higher grades on the post-test" (p. 3). So, if the intention of the initial assessment is to determine what students are bringing to class in terms of dispositions, unique characteristics, and learning opportunities, then the initial assessment must not be a test.

Development of Initial Assessments

There are guidelines to consider in developing initial assessments that help educators diagnose and discover. Following these guidelines ensures that learners are not discouraged and deceived. Guskey and McTighe's work (2016) provides us with guidelines for the development of initial assessments. They are:

1. Clarify the purpose(s) for the initial assessment. This purpose should come directly from the learning intentions and success criteria. The learning intentions and success criteria should lead directly to the initial assessments. What do learners already know, understand, and what are they able to do prior to the lessons?

2. Determine how you will use the information. When learners engage in an initial assessment, what will the information be used for? What role will this evidence play in the next decision about teaching and learning? If we plan on going about business as usual (e.g., per the pacing guide), then the initial assessment is a waste of time.

3. Use initial assessments judiciously and efficiently. Design initial assessments so that they provide quick and readily accessible evidence to both teachers and students. If the initial assessment cannot inform the immediate next steps, we should reconsider the initial assessment.

Clarifying the purposes of initial assessments serves to keep learners informed as to the reasoning or "why" behind our assessment. Mr. Lee is a high school social studies teacher who has devoted a lot of energy to making sure his learners understand the "why" behind initial assessments. "Once my learners participate in a task, say, responding to a particular Supreme Court decision, we debrief the task by developing a list of 'Things I Need to Know' that would have helped me better respond to the Court's decision." Mr. Lee, by modeling evaluative thinking, has emphasized the purpose of the initial assessment and then used the evidence to collaboratively develop guiding or driving questions for the next steps in his students' learning about judicial review. As we consider the reasoning behind the initial assessments, collaborating with our learners models the value of not knowing, yet. Mr. Lee is highlighting the importance of mistakes and helping his learners recognize where they are going next in their learning as well as providing them ways to monitor progress. Mr. Lee often thanks them by "letting them know that this assessment helps me better understand their thinking and promising to change our plans for moving forward based on where I can be of most help as their teacher." Mr. Lee knows how he is going to use the information gathered from the initial assessment before he ever engages learners in the task.

Our initial assessments should be used judiciously and efficiently. Initial assessments need to be used when "results cannot be predicted and when the exercise provides clear benefits to students" (Guskey & McTighe, 2016, p. 42). If initial assessments are created with the learning intentions and success criteria in mind, that is truly when we can employ initial assessments with impact. The information they provide helps us capture the skill, will, and thrill of our learners.

Teacher Noticing

Mr. Kim has provided his learners with several different weighted marbles, plastic malleable track, and other supplies (e.g., protractor, rule, calculator, and graphing paper) at their laboratory stations. He introduces the task at hand by getting their attention and sharing the following prompt: "Over the next several days we are learning about the relationships between different variables in projectile motion. Your task is to use as little or as many of the available supplies at your laboratory benches." Mr. Kim has designed and implemented this mini-laboratory as an initial assessment on two-dimensional or projectile motion. However, the rationale for using this task as an initial assessment may be difficult for some of us to see. We may look at this and, when weighing this decision against a more traditional paper-pencil initial assessment, ask how this is going to tell Mr. Kim what his learners know and do not know. An entrance ticket, set of multiple-choice questions, or a paper-pencil problem set would work better in this situation, right? The answer to this question has to do with what Mr. Kim notices during this task.

Teacher noticing is the active process of attending to what is happening in a particular learning task or activity and then interpreting what we see. For Mr. Kim, his noticing requires that he notice what learners are doing during the mini-laboratory and then he must interpret those actions through the lens of where his learners are going. From the perspective of teacher noticing, the question of how is this mini-laboratory going to provide the information Mr. Kim needs is actually the wrong question to ask. Instead, we should be asking the following questions of Mr. Kim and ourselves (adapted from Sherin, Jacobs, & Philipp, 2011):

- What are we noticing about students as they engage in learning tasks?
- What does this tell me about their current dispositions, unique characteristics, and learning opportunities?

From Ms. Henry to Mr. Kim, analyzing standards, designing and implementing initial assessments, and then having your learners take part in those assessments is not a stopping point. An initial assessment is only as good as the evidence it gathers about students' prior knowledge, motivations, and willingness to learn. Furthermore, that evidence is only worthwhile if we notice what is needed to move learning forward. Those that are better at teacher noticing, often referred to as *expert noticing*, are quicker at identify situations that need an intervention, recognize when a new approach to teaching is needed, better incorporate student interests and motivations into teaching, chunk and pace the learning through the learning progression, and recognize when learners have truly got it (Schoenfeld, 2011). In fact, Schoenfeld (2011) suggested that expert noticers devote more of their time to what he calls "diagnostic teaching" rather than behavior management. So, what goes into Ms. Henry's and Mr. Kim's noticing so that what they notice truly informs their sense-making about student prior knowledge, motivations, and willingness to learn? What allows them to engage in diagnostic teaching?

First, to engage in diagnostic teaching, we must have strong knowledge of the content and skills students are expected to learn. Beyond analyzing the standard, we must have the necessary content knowledge to understand what proficiency and mastery look like in sums and differences, two-dimensional motion, and globalization, for example. This requires us to draw on our own content knowledge as teachers within the particular domain associated with the new learning. With regard to new learning, we also have to see learning from the learners' perspective and recognize how they are most likely to approach the content (Ball & Bass, 2009). Figure 2.4 helps show this relationship.

For Ms. Henry, this means she needs to not only anticipate, but recognize when a learner simply rearranges the numbers instead of regrouping. If a learner says that 43 – 27 = 24, he or she simply flipped 3 and 7 to make sure the smaller number was subtracted from the larger number. Mr. Kim has to recognize that learners may not see the relationship between dropping the steel marble and using the plastic ramp as both being projectile motion. Teacher noticing, and thus diagnostic teaching, requires educators to blend their content knowledge with learners' novice approaches to content so that teachers can spot students' current level of understanding.

To get the most from our standards and initial assessments, we have to engage in teacher noticing through evaluative thinking

Figure 2.4 Two components of teacher noticing

and reflecting on our teaching. Teacher noticing requires that we are selective about what we notice and purposefully overlook. This means we have to approach any learning experience, face-to-face or remote, aware of what we are looking for from our learners so that we are not distracted by those things that are not directly related to assessing what learners know, understand, and are able to do. For example, if learners cooperatively work to identify character traits from a text and then support their thinking with evidence from the text, focusing on whether learners are seated at their desks versus standing will inhibit our ability to engage in diagnostic teaching about their understanding of character traits and the skill of using evidence from text. Along those same lines, we cannot possibly process everything that is going on in a single learning task or activity with every learner. For a class of 30 students, we must engage in quick scans that intentionally seek the essential knowledge, skills, and understandings extracted from the standard. These quick scans should also seek to recognize when learners are demonstrating a solid understanding of a concept. Catching students being successful is just as important as identifying gaps in knowing where they are in their learning.

What both Ms. Henry and Mr. Kim demonstrate is that they have:

1. Thought carefully about the expectations for their learners and the specific content they are expected to know, understand, and be able to do.

2. Developed an initial assessment that would generate multiple sources of evidence around this content.

3. Capitalized on their own content knowledge in these areas to carefully notice their students' thinking.

4. Established a continuous sense of this demonstrated thinking to better understand where their students are in their learning.

By selecting the specific initial assessment to gather this evidence, Ms. Henry and Mr. Kim provide multiple opportunities for their learners to show not only their content knowledge, but their dispositions about the learning. In general, this allows us to pull together all of this evidence, incorporating behavioral and social-emotional factors, to diagnose and discover the presence of a gap and the nature of that gap. If we notice specific aspects of their dispositions, the gap may not be related to knowledge or skill, but motivation. If we notice aspects of our learners' skill sets, the gap may not be related to motivation or knowledge, but require the deliberate practice of a specific skill. Lastly, if we notice aspects of our learners' knowledge base, the gap may not be related to skills or motivation.

This gap, then, represents the skill, will, and thrill of our learners. As Hattie and Donoghue (2016) point out,

> *The skill, will and thrill can intertwine during learning and that these three inputs are also important outcomes of learning—the aim is to enhance the will (e.g., the willingness to reinvest in more and deeper learning), the thrill (e.g., the emotions associated with successful learning, the curiosity and the willingness to explore what one does not know) and the skills (e.g., the content and the deeper understanding). (p. 9)*

Diagnosing and discovering who is in our schools and learning environments represents the first part of closing the gap between design and execution, intention and potential to implementation. At the onset of this component, this may appear to be a very daunting task. But what we hope we have done in this chapter is break down diagnosing and discovering into its essential elements:

1. Analyze the national and local standards to understand the expectations around what learners must know, understand, and be able to do within that framework.

2. Design and implement initial assessments that diagnose and discover gaps in student knowledge, skills, and understandings.

3. Use expert teacher noticing to attend to student responses surrounding those initial assessments and make sense of that information.

Once we have evidence about where learners are now, our purpose—our goal, our own skill, will, and thrill—is to make decisions about what intervention will "enhance the will, the thrill, and skills" of our learners.

"

Appropriate interventions or instructional
actions are identified based on the diagnosis
and discovery phase.

3

CHAPTER 3

INTERVENTION

Figure 3.1 The DIIE model

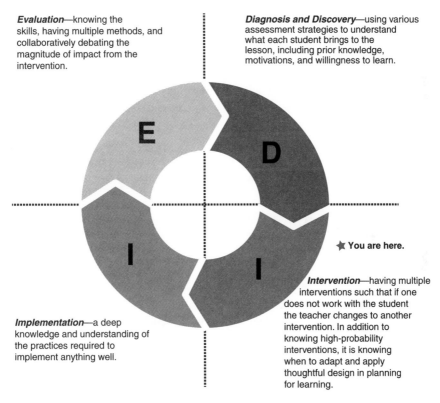

Evaluation—knowing the skills, having multiple methods, and collaboratively debating the magnitude of impact from the intervention.

Diagnosis and Discovery—using various assessment strategies to understand what each student brings to the lesson, including prior knowledge, motivations, and willingness to learn.

★ You are here.

Intervention—having multiple interventions such that if one does not work with the student the teacher changes to another intervention. In addition to knowing high-probability interventions, it is knowing when to adapt and apply thoughtful design in planning for learning.

Implementation—a deep knowledge and understanding of the practices required to implement anything well.

Intervening requires identifying and selecting the right, high-probability tools that move student learning forward. Doing so ensures students acquire and consolidate content, skills, and understanding. Appropriate interventions or instructional actions are identified based on the diagnosis and discovery phase, allowing teachers to identify students' current levels of understanding and the goals for learning. The evidence is generated from initial assessments that allow us to make the best decisions about how

Figure 3.2 Teacher noticing moves us to act

Teacher Noticing **+** Teacher Action **=** Impact on Student Learning

---

Appropriate interventions or instructional actions are identified based on the diagnosis and discovery phase, allowing teachers to identify students' current levels of understanding and the goals for learning.

to close the gap between where learners are now and where we are going in the learning (see Figure 3.2). This brings us to the discussion of how to close the gap. Simply put, what makes teachers' expert noticing so powerful is that we act upon the things that we notice.

For example, if we notice a gap in learners' prior knowledge about place value or cellular processes, their disposition toward the study of ancient civilizations, or their motivation to engage in independent reading a fictional text, our decision to act on that—noticing in a way that moves learning forward and closes the knowledge gap—is what produces the impact on student learning. In doing so, we serve our purpose as change agents. However, if we do not possess the content or pedagogical knowledge to act, then the value in analyzing standards, designing and implementing initial assessments, and gathering that evidence is lost.

This Is Not Deficit Thinking

Before we move any further in this discussion, we want to address a possible misconception that could arise from this process: deficit thinking. Without any intention to do so, we could easily begin to approach each unit, lesson, or task with the mindset or assumption that our learners have a deficit that we must locate and fix. This is absolutely not what the DIIE model is designed to do. In fact, this approach advocates for and supports the exact opposite. The Goldilocks principle should govern our teaching and learning at all times: "not too easy, not too hard, and not too boring." This principle should apply for all knowledge, dispositions, and motivations. Let's examine how Ms. Rodriguez uses initial assessments to determine the nature of the learning for her students.

Lelia Rodriguez teaches English literature in a Royal Grammar School outside of London. Her focus over the next several days is an analysis of Shakespeare's *Hamlet* found in their textbooks. She recognizes that the standards focus on the literary analysis through the lens of the specific time period during which the author lived and produced his or her writings. Focusing on literary heritage, she will, in the end, help her learners see how this has influenced modern works in literature. To get started though, she has designed an initial task that she hopes will engage her learners in the life and times of William Shakespeare. Based on what her students need to know, she identified jigsaw as an appropriate task. This initial task will also provide evidence allowing her to make the best decisions about where to go next in the learning. "I was not surprised by how little they knew about Shakespeare—having heard about him their entire lives, they had developed a view of him that was quite full of historical inaccuracies." Upon further discussion with Ms. Rodriquez, she also pointed out that there was a very different tone about the content. "I was a bit taken aback by their lack of confidence in being able to comprehend the works of Mr. Shakespeare. Plus, they did not demonstrate much motivation toward this particular learning. This brought about a bit of challenge and will require me to think about how to proceed."

Although Ms. Rodriguez notices that there are gaps in her learners' prior knowledge, dispositions, and motivation, simply noticing this does not suffice in moving from ideation to implementation. The main idea behind intervention in the DIIE model is this: Once we notice, we must act. And, we have to act with high-probability interventions that have the most impact on student learning; this occurs through the acquisition and consolidation of learning across skill, will, and thrill. Ms. Rodriguez's effective and efficient action is a function of resources, goals, and orientation. As Figure 3.3 helps illustrate, the resources for those decisions are the multiple interventions available to us as teachers. In addition to knowing multiple, high-quality interventions, we have to know how to align and adapt those interventions to the specific needs of our learners with the goal of moving learning forward. After all, we are the change agents.

Ms. Rodriguez has diagnosed and discovered gaps. Let's look closer at these gaps so that we can better understand what resources, or

Figure 3.3 The essential parts of intervening

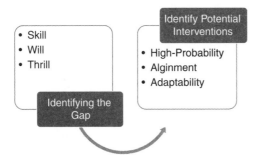

interventions, are available to us. With this, we can align to and close the various gaps in learners' skill, will, and thrill.

Identifying the Skill, Will, and Thrill: Where Are Our Learners Now?

As we have noted before, the diagnosis and discovery component of the DIIE model involves understanding learners' dispositions, unique characteristics, and learning opportunities. We need to know more than whether or not students can regroup to solve two-digit subtraction problems, define symbolic representation in literature, or describe judicial review by the Supreme Court of the United States. Again, we have tried to emphasize that when looking at the DIIE cycle, teachers must diagnose and discover multiple aspects about their learners before moving forward with teaching and learning. We want to spend time conceptualizing a way to think about these aspects. In other words, we have established the expectations for learners, developed clear and useful initial assessments, and attended to the evidence generated by those initial assessments. Now what? Well, we have to take that evidence and define the gap. The gap could relate to, but is not limited to, *prior knowledge, dispositions, or motivations*. With all of the evidence we have, how do we make sense of the gap? The gap, or distance between where learners are now and the expectations for where they are going, can be classified into three broad categories: skill, will, and thrill.

Skill. Hattie and Donoghue (2016) refer to *skill* as "the prior achievement students bring to the task" (p. 2). Expanding on this definition, this aspect of the gap involves knowledge, skills, and/or understandings related to the content.

> Skill refers to what the learner already knows, understands, and is able to do. Often described as background or prior knowledge, this is the content, skills, and understanding students bring to the new learning.

This information about our learners comes from our understanding what experiences students are bringing into the learning environment and how they made meaning of those experiences. Content knowledge is an important aspect of skill. For example, when Javier Colton walks into physics class for the very first time, his knowledge of measurement, units, fluids, forces, and energy comes from his many years working with his father at their family-owned collision repair shop. Not only does Javier have a vast understanding of the content, he also has developed proficiency in the processes and practices commonly taught in high school science classes. Maria Sanchez has lived all over the world. She comes from

The gap, or distance between where learners are now and the expectations for where they are going, can be classified into three broad categories: skill, will, and thrill.

a military family and has had the opportunity to experience many cultures from Eastern Europe to South East Asia. She is fluent in more than one language and knows how to navigate diverse social situations. She has the content knowledge found in high school human geography classes and the social-emotional skills to work collaboratively with each of her peers. Equally important to content knowledge are aspects of beliefs, working memory, and expectations from the student's home and culture. Being able to access this wealth of information will allow us to have a greater impact on a student's learning.

On the other hand, knowing where learners need additional support is equally valuable. Not everyone will have the same *skill* (i.e., knowledge, skills, and understanding) as Javier and Maria. So, as we make sense of the evidence gathered during the diagnose and discovery component and decide what action to take; this requires that we ask the following reflective questions:

- What is the knowledge base of my learners? Does this call for adaptive or compensatory approaches to the learning?

- What skills, related to the content, do my learners bring to this topic? What additional support is needed in developing or applying these skills?

- Finally, do my learners need additional support in developing academic language that will allow them to engage in academic discourse?

The answers to these questions will allow us to act on our diagnosis and discovery by identifying specific high-probability interventions that will help learners acquire and consolidate their learning of knowledge, skills, and understandings.

> Knowing when to focus on skill requires us to diagnose whether the learner has a gap in his or her knowledge base, skill set, or essential understanding that would hinder him or her from moving forward in the new learning.

Will. The *will* that our learners bring to the learning environment involves the dispositions they have toward the learning and the associated implications for our teaching. Another way to look at the will is to consider the personalities our students bring to class.

> Will refers to a learner's disposition toward learning. These dispositions reflect how the learner responds to specific learning situations such as their inclination to engage and then persist in a learning experience or task.

Fostering opportunities where students can say to themselves "I want to do this" is how we build the will of the learner. Jackson Thomas finds value in tasks that allow him to create. He wants to work in the arts and will turn anything into a song, painting, or dance. Likewise, he is fascinated by the role of art in understanding history, sociology, and the psychology of human kind. For Jackson, it is a struggle to engage in the sciences or mathematics unless the particular topic can be tied to art. For example, he decided to create a piece of art solely from mathematical equations. His teacher, Ms. Evelyn Babers, recalls this particular exercise as "a completely out of left field response to the assignment. I wanted them to demonstrate that they understood transformations. Instead, he developed a replica of a Mondrian painting using linear equations." On the other hand, his sister, Tessa Thomas, wants to be a marine biologist. She approached a similar assignment with a very different take. "I just want to get it done so that I can go back to reading about dolphins and the loss of their habitats. I don't see how this is going to help me become a marine biologist."

The will of these two learners requires that their teachers make different decisions about the interventions needed to keep moving forward in their learning. From the perspective of *will*, when we make sense of the evidence gathered during the diagnose and discovery component of the DIIE model, we have to ask:

- What do I know about my learners' interests and dispositions that I can use to leverage or enhance their intrinsic motivation?

- Do I need to provide additional support to help my learners self-regulate their focus?

- Do I need to provide additional support to help my learners develop tools, strategies, or habits that will move their learning forward?

The answers to these questions will allow us to act on our diagnosis and discovery by identifying specific high-probability interventions that will help learners acquire and consolidate their learning by influencing students' level of confidence and self-efficacy.

Knowing when to focus on the will of a learner requires us to diagnose whether the learner is willing to engage in learning, demonstrate resourcefulness in working through a learning experience or task, and strategically persist in that experience or task.

Thrill. Perhaps the most powerful driving force for learning is the *thrill* of learning.

> Thrill refers to the learner's motivation—why they want to engage in the learning experience or task.

Think back to those learning experiences or tasks that have stuck with you throughout your entire life. Was the experience around a particular book? Do you recall a particular mathematics problem, science laboratory, musical performance, or historical event? The thrill provided elaborate encoding of that experience or task in your brain, making recall very easy. In fact, the recall likely involves most of your senses. You may even be able to remember what you wore on that day. Danielle Miller recalls her high school capstone project where she worked with large farm animals at a local veterinary hospital. That experience, which she can recall with jaw-dropping detail, cemented her ambitions of becoming a large animal veterinarian. On a smaller, but no less important, scale comes a recollection from Ava Bradley when she received feedback on an eighth-grade mathematics test. "I spent a lot of time practicing. Every day. Math has not always been easy for me, but my teacher kept telling me that I had it in me. I spent time each day reviewing for the test; practice problems, explaining it to my friends, my siblings. I will never forget the look on Mr. Showalter's face when he handed my paper back and I had not made a single mistake. I get goosebumps telling the story. I knew right then and there that I had it in me to do this every time. Well, if I worked at it, anyway."

Thrill often involves students taking action and creating something, using the knowledge they gained previously. In many cases, there is some level of choice in the products that create thrill. From the perspective of *thrill*, when we make sense of the evidence gathered during the diagnose and discovery component of the DIIE model, we have to ask:

- How do I design an environment that offers my learners the opportunity to experience the thrill of learning?

- What tasks will allow students an opportunity to take action based on the knowledge they have gained?

> Knowing when to focus on the thrill of a learner requires us to discover an understanding of his or her motivation. If learners are motivated to develop understanding and make meaning of their learning, there is less of a need to focus on thrill than when learners simply aim to regurgitate facts back without understanding. This is often evidenced by learners putting in minimal effort for maximum return.

Applying the Goldilocks Principle

Let's quickly return to Ms. Rodriguez's classroom and her initial assessment. As her secondary learners engaged in the jigsaw, what if they would have demonstrated a high level of prior knowledge, a strong sense of confidence or self-efficacy in reading and analyzing *Hamlet*, and the motivation to learn more? She recognized this in some of her learners. "There were many of my students that had significant amounts of knowledge about Mr. Shakespeare and, in particular *Hamlet*. And, they were quite keen on the idea of learning more about his works."

For these learners, there does not appear to be a gap in their skill, will, or thrill for the level of expectations outlined in the standards. Ms. Rodriguez's initial assessment provided this valuable information, suggesting that these learners need to have the "bar raised" on their learning. In other words, if some of her learners have already arrived at where the standard said they were going, we have to provide a new destination. Where are they going next?

Ms. Rodriquez will need to adapt the teaching and learning during this particular unit of study to ensure that the learners are engaged in the right level of challenge: "not too easy, not too hard, and not too boring." We will devote a significant amount of time to this particular situation when we get to implementation in the next chapter. For now, we want to acknowledge there will be times when initial assessments will determine that adjustments need to be made in the learning environment in order to maintain the Goldilocks principle.

Focusing on skill, will, and thrill is not a linear or sequential process. In fact, there is no algorithm or if-then loop for knowing when to focus on one over the other or move from one to the other. This requires constant monitoring of where learners are, what interventions are available, and whether or not the implementation of these interventions makes a difference. We will address implementation and evaluation in the upcoming chapters. For now, let's look at interventions that have a high probability of impacting skill, will, and thrill.

High-Probability Interventions

High-probability interventions are *what work best* in teaching and learning. These interventions are part of the Visible Learning+™ database and are derived from the key findings from *Visible Learning* (Hattie, 2009). One of those key findings is that *there is no one way to teach or any best instructional strategy that works in all situations for all students*. We must select the right high-probability intervention that moves student learning forward through the acquisition and consolidation of content, skills, and understandings. When the intervention aligns with the diagnosis of where learners are, there is compelling evidence for certain strategies and approaches that have a greater likelihood of helping students reach their learning goals. Visible Learning+, and therefore the high-probability interventions, is based on effect size information that has been collected and analyzed over many years to inform how we transform the findings from the Visible Learning+ research into learning experiences and challenging tasks that are most likely to have the strongest influence on student learning.

High-probability interventions are *what work best* in teaching and learning.

Aligning High-Probability Interventions With Skill, Will, and Thrill

Intervening is more than just knowing high-probability interventions. In addition to having these strategies or approaches as resources, we must select the right, high-probability interventions that move student learning forward and, at the same time, enhance their disposition about, and motivation for, learning. There are specific interventions that have a strong influence on skill, but not on the will and thrill. Similarly, there are specific interventions that have strong influence on the will or thrill of learners, but not on their skills. The timing of the intervention matters. Let's look at specific high-probability interventions and where they can be leveraged to potentially maximize learning for our students—we say "potentially" because we still have to implement these interventions, which will be addressed in the next chapter. For now, we are still focused on the first "I" in the DIIE model.

High-Probability Interventions for Enhancing Skill

When students walk into our classrooms or log onto our remote learning environments, they bring with them prior knowledge generated from their prior experiences inside and outside of our class. Ms. Aguilar fully acknowledges that her learners' prior experiences in the study of history strongly influence their skill, and thus her decisions about the teaching and learning of ancient civilizations. "They often come in with a very fact-based view of history. They rattle off dates and names, without the skill of thinking like historians. These learners are capable, but need specific strategies and approaches that build these skills. For others, they have these skills from different prior experiences and my focus is to keep them moving forward." For Ms. Aguilar, prior experiences, and therefore, prior knowledge is related to both content, skills, and understandings. Our focus as teachers is to use evaluative thinking and make intentional, purposeful, and deliberate decisions about what knowledge, skills, and understandings need to be in place for learners to successfully engage in the new learning. We can do this by engaging in content and cognitive task analysis.

Content and cognitive task analysis is the process in which we examine standards and skill objectives to break them down into progressive components (Szidon & Franzone, 2009). Cognitive task analysis requires the deconstruction of specific outcomes articulated in national or local standards. Let's return to our example in the previous chapter on globalization.

General Outcome

Students will explore the impacts of globalization on their lives.

Specific Outcomes

Values and Attitudes

Students will:

1.1 acknowledge and appreciate the existence of multiple perspectives in a globalizing world.

1.2 appreciate why peoples in Canada and other locations strive to promote their cultures, languages, and identities in a globalizing world.

1.3 appreciate how identities and cultures shape, and are shaped by, globalization.

Knowledge and Understanding

Students will:

1.4 explore ways in which individuals and collectives express identities (traditions, language, religion, spirituality, the arts, attire, relationship to land, ideological beliefs, role modeling).

Source: Alberta Learning. (2007). *Social Studies 10-1* [Program of Studies]. Edmonton, Canada: Alberta Learning.

Standards establish what our students will *need to know* and help us avoid being distracted by what is *neat for them to know*. For this specific example, for learners to "explore the impacts of globalization on their lives," what prior knowledge is assumed in listing the concepts or nouns from this standard? What will students need to know, understand, and be able to do in order to engage in this new learning? We can break apart our complex standards into more palpable, bite-sized chunks for our students. Looking at a specific statement in the standard, "appreciate how identities and cultures shape, and are shaped by, globalization," learners must have prior knowledge around the concepts of identity, culture, and most important, globalization. Notice that this specific standard does not state that learners can define or describe globalization. This is assumed prior knowledge or learning. Thus, we have to ensure this content has been acquired, consolidated, and retrievable.

Once we have determined the necessary elements of the standards, students need to then engage in the new learning. If their background knowledge is insufficient for them to successfully engage in the new learning, this will need to be addressed using high-probability interventions. These interventions include (Hattie & Donoghue, 2016):

- Vocabulary programs to build academic language

- Summarizing

- Elaborate interrogation

- Direct instruction to build and support the acquisition of specific knowledge

- Deliberate practice to support the consolidation of this specific knowledge

- Rehearsal and memorization to support ease in retrieving this specific knowledge

- Effective feedback about the learning

- Spaced versus massed practice to maintain this learning

Table 3.1 provides the average effect size, as well as a brief definition for each of these interventions. As new research is added to the Visible Learning database, these effect sizes may change. Visible Learning Meta X provides the latest values for each of the effect sizes in the following tables. A complete list

Table 3.1   High-probability interventions for enhancing learners' skill

Intervention	Average Effect Size	Description
Vocabulary Programs	0.63	Vocabulary programs build the vocabulary, subject matter vocabulary, and make connections to other words.
Summarizing	0.74	The ability to summarize a text is often taken as a marker of reading comprehension, and for this reason many scholars have advocated explicit summarization training for students who struggle with comprehension. This can include deleting unnecessary material, deleting material that is redundant, substituting a subordinate term for a list of items or actions, selecting a topic sentence, and constructing a topic if one is only implicitly suggested by the text.

(Continued)

Table 3.1 (Continued)

Intervention	Average Effect Size	Description
Elaborate Interrogation	0.56	This questioning technique calls for readers to generate an explanation for an explicitly stated fact by asking questions such as: "Why is this true?"; "Why does this make sense?"; or even simply "Why?" Unlike more typical textbook questions—which ask "what" instead of "why"—elaborative interrogation has been shown to promote learning from texts.
Direct Instruction	0.59	Direct instruction refers to instructional approaches that are structured, sequenced, and led by teachers. Direct instruction requires teachers to have clear learning intentions and success criteria, building a commitment and engagement among the students in the learning task; use modeling and checking for understanding in their teaching; and engage in guided practice so that every student can demonstrate his or her grasp of new learning by working through an activity or exercise under the teacher's direct supervision.
Deliberate Practice	0.79	This learning technique involves extensive engagement in relevant practice activities in order to improve particular aspects of performance. Deliberate practice often refers to challenging, effortful repetition, often adjusted through feedback. While regular practice can include much repetition, deliberate practice requires focused attention and is conducted with the specific goal of improving performance.
Rehearsal and Memorization	0.73	Rehearsal is a term used by memory researchers to refer to mental techniques for helping us remember information. It can involve many strategies such as repeating information to be memorized by organizing it at random and repeating the information when prompted by a visual cue, such as an index card or photograph.
Effective Feedback	0.64	Feedback in learning can be defined as information allowing a learner to reduce the gap between where they are in their learning and the expectation for where they are going in their learning. Specifically, feedback is information provided by an agent (e.g., teacher, peer, book, parent, self/experience) regarding aspects of one's performance or understanding that reduces the discrepancy between what is understood and what is aimed to be understood.
Spaced Versus Massed Practice	0.65	The claim is that students are better able to commit information to memory when they study that information in spaced (or distributed) intervals rather than all at once in a "massed" interval. Spaced practices involve practice broken up into a number of shorter sessions, over a longer period of time. Massed practice consists of fewer, longer training sessions.

of influences can be found on Visible Learning MetaX (https://www.visiblelearningmetax.com/) which updates effect sizes regularly.

These specific high-probability interventions are noted for supporting learners to build the background knowledge necessary for the level of skill needed to engage new learning. As we move toward implementation, one of the questions we will address is what to do if learners already have the skills necessary to engage in the new learning. The answer is to dive right into the new learning.

High-Probability Interventions for Enhancing Will

Ms. DeLoach, as part of her school's "what makes a good learner" plan, strives to create learning opportunities for both skill and learners' dispositions toward learning. "In addition to teaching about forces and motions, I want them to approach phenomenon in science by reflecting on their work using the worked examples or exemplars. I want them to have an internal dialogue running in their mind that guides them in monitoring their own learning progress." For Ms. DeLoach, it is important to explicitly teach the dispositions that are associated with the greatest gains in learning. Not only should learners acquire and consolidate learning, we must support their journey in becoming assessment-capable visible learners, or learners that have the tools they need to move their own learning forward, monitor their learning progress, and make adjustments when necessary. "In a remote learning environment, I spend time providing opportunities for my learners to reflect on their learning and justify their approach to learning." We all must take steps to explicitly foster high impact learning dispositions just as Ms. DeLoach has done in her remote science classroom. Learners will likely approach our learning environments, tasks, and activities with very different dispositions toward learning. These learners are positive, negative, productive, and disruptive. Just as Ms. DeLoach has goals for her learners around forces and motion, she also has goals for their tendencies to respond to new and challenging learning. We should actively take these steps with our learners by promoting the following:

- Self-regulation strategies
- Self-judgement and reflection
- Metacognition strategies
- Strategy monitoring
- Transfer strategies
- Detecting similarities and differences
- Practice testing

We can create a purposeful learning environment where students use metacognitive strategies, among other interventions listed to promote an internal dialogue—a key characteristic of assessment-capable learners.

Table 3.2 provides the average effect size, as well as a brief definition for each of these interventions. Again, these values may change. A complete list of influences can be found on Visible Learning MetaX (https://www .visiblelearningmetax.com/) which updates effect sizes regularly.

Table 3.2 High-probability interventions for enhancing learners' will

Intervention	Average Effect Size	Description
Self-Regulation Strategies	0.52	A self-regulated learner requires motivation (for instance, to attempt to solve a math problem), cognition (to think through the problem), and metacognition (to review whether they are performing the task correctly).
Self-Judgement and Reflection	0.75	Self-judgement is a critical component of independent, self-directed learning, and yet students can often over- or underestimate their own capabilities. Teachers should strive to cultivate in students the ability to dispassionately apply established standards to their own work. There is a high value in a student's ability to reflect on his or her work, discern its relationship to established standards, and make self-judgements.
Metacognition Strategies	0.58	Metacognition is thinking about thinking; it includes methods used to help students understand the way they learn.
Strategy Monitoring	0.58	A metacognitive practice occurs when a student monitors her or his own strategies to complete a task. It often involves students being trained both in problem-solving techniques and in monitoring techniques (through which they observe how and whether they are following problem-solving protocols).
Transfer Strategies	0.86	For learning to be effective, students must be able to make a spontaneous, unprompted, and appropriate transfer of a learning or problem-solving strategy from one context to another. This can be near transfer to new problems similar to the instruction, or far transfer to new situations and domains.
Practice Testing	0.46	Practice testing is a well-established strategy for improving student learning. The aim of practice testing is to support long-term retention and increase access to retrieving the "to-be-remembered" information. It is sometimes called retrieval practice, practice testing, or test-enhanced learning.

High-Probability Interventions for Enhancing Thrill

The prior knowledge and experiences that students bring with them not only have an impact on their skills, but can also impact their motivations. Whether through face-to-face, hybrid, or virtual learning, learners will approach the learning experience with a variety of motivations. As teachers, we are tasked with providing learning opportunities and interventions that will foster intrinsic motivation so that learners will engage in the experiences and tasks in such a way that they experience both growth and achievement. Before delving into examples of these interventions, it is important to differentiate between the different types of motivations, because they have different effects on student learning and are *not all positively associated with thrill*. These influences should thus be a focus for us as teachers, and are as follows:

- Motivation
- Surface motivation and approach
- Deep motivation and approach
- Achieving or strategic motivation and approach

At first glance, some of these effect sizes may appear surprising to us. To make sense of these effect sizes, we have to understand each type of motivation and how they inform our choice of intervention. For example, what interventions support learners in the development of deep motivation and not surface motivation? To answer this question, let's look at these two types of motivation. The difference between surface and deep motivations is discrepant enough to warrant an explanation. For example, Ms. Leonard, a third-grade teacher in the United States, attests to how surface-motivated learners approach their learning. "I have some learners that just want to get the information and repeat it back to me. They do not give much attention to understanding the content." The result is not the acquisition or consolidation of learning—it is simply compliance and task completion. Learning therefore suffers. Whereas, deep motivation drives learners to seek and aim for mastery, deeper understanding. "These learners show a higher degree of investment in not just completing the task, but understanding what they are learning, why they are learning it, and what successful learning looks and feels like," explains Ms. Leonard. Those learners that are driven by achieving motivation move between the two, depending on their own goals. Ms. Leonard describes them as "learners that are comfortable with simply getting their mathematics done so that they can devote more time, effort, and energy to their STEM projects or reading their good choice books." This motivation involves students being strategic in their motivation—choosing when to be surface learners and understand the knowledge, when to go deep and investigate relations, when to master, and when to perform to the satisfaction of others (teachers, peers, family).

Any intervention we choose to apply through strategies in our learning environments should focus on the development of deep motivation, and approaches with the intention our students know when to apply the strategies of achieving motivation. Once we have determined the specific motivations that we intend to foster with our students, we can build on that motivation by increasing our learners (Hattie & Donoghue, 2016):

- Self-efficacy/self-concept
- Task value
- The right level of challenge
- Success criteria

We can create a learning environment and engage in specific interactions with our students that enhances their self-efficacy and the perceived value of the learning tasks.

Table 3.3 provides the average effect size, as well as a brief definition for each of these interventions. Continue to check these effect sizes for updates using the Visible Learning Meta X database (https://www.visiblelearningmetax.com/) which updates effect sizes regularly.

Table 3.3 High-probability interventions for enhancing learners' thrill

Intervention	Average Effect Size	Description
Self-Efficacy	0.71	First theorized in educational theory by Albert Bandura, "self-efficacy" refers to a sense of confidence or the set of self-perceptions that influence thought, actions, and emotional arousal by enabling people to make decisions about what course of action they intend to pursue.
Task Value	0.46	The student's perception that a particular task has value shapes his or her willingness to seek help, to exert effort, and to manage his or her own feelings of anxiety. Task value is a function of four components: (1) interest (the enjoyment one gets from engaging in the task), (2) utility value (the instrumental value of the task or activity for helping to fulfill another short- or long-range goal), (3) attainment value (the link between the task and one's sense of self and either personal or social identity), and (4) cost (what may be given up by making a specific choice or the negative experiences associated with each possible choice).
Self-Verbalization and Self-Questioning	0.59	Self-verbalization (talking to oneself about a difficult intellectual task) and self-questioning (interrogating oneself about the information one encounters) are both cognitive tools, and both have been associated with higher levels of understanding. Indeed, numerous studies have directed students to ask themselves different types of questions while reading (higher-order questions about meaning, self-monitoring questions about the reading process, or questions about relevant prior knowledge).

Right Level of Challenge	0.59	A necessary precondition for meaningful learning, appropriately challenging goals provide the preconditions for student engagement and the development of intrinsic motivation. Numerous scholars have suggested that students thrive most when teachers describe clearly the ultimate goals of a particular course of instruction, and when they formulate such goals to be challenging but achievable. The Goldilocks principle of challenge is not too hard, not too easy, and not too boring.
Success Criteria	0.88	Success criteria are the standards by which the project will be judged at the end to decide whether or not it has been successful. They are often brief, co-constructed with students, aim to remind students of those aspects on which they need to focus, and can relate to the surface (content, ideas) and deep (relations, transfer) learnings from the lesson(s).

For this first "I" of the DIIE model, intervening, we should use the information from diagnosing and discovering to identify and select the right high-probability intervention that moves student learning forward through the acquisition and consolidation of content, skills, and understanding. This requires that we also identify interventions that will support learners' will and thrill. Skill is the content, skills, and understanding; will is the motivation and application of those skills; thrill is the disposition to use this learning later, in different contexts. The specific examples discussed in this chapter are just a sample from over 200 interventions that have the potential to accelerate student learning. Yet, having these interventions as resources for moving from potential to implementation is only part of the process. We have to identify the intervention that *works best* for the specific focus: skill, will, or thrill. But, we are not quite done.

We do not make students come to school because they know and understand already; indeed they come to school to learn that which they are yet to know—our role is opening the excitement of precious knowledge and understanding, to invite students to more deeply know and master topics and ideas that have enthralled us, and to light the spark of their own learning. As you have likely noticed, the DIIE model acknowledges this pursuit, and the premise is that we are so much more successful in teaching when we understand the starting points of our students, when we use evidence to make decisions about optimal interventions, and when we are closely attuned to the quality of the implementation of these interventions. This requires much skill and expertise, and we continue to marvel at the excellence that is all around us in the teaching profession.

The next step is implementing that intervention into our learning environment. An intervention is only as good as our implementation, and that requires us to adapt the intervention to reflect who we teach and our specific learning mode—the local context of our learning environment (e.g., face-to-face, hybrid, and remote learning).

An intervention is only as good as our implementation and that requires us to adapt the intervention to reflect who we teach and our specific learning mode—the local context of our learning environment (e.g., face-to-face, hybrid, and remote learning).

"
Implementation demands that we take each
high-probability intervention and adapt that
intervention to reflect the context of our own
learning environment.

4

CHAPTER 4

IMPLEMENTATION

Figure 4.1 The DIIE model

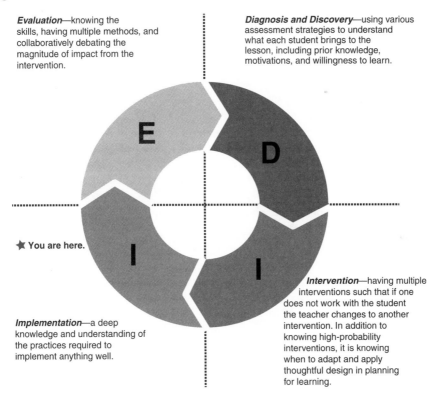

Evaluation—knowing the skills, having multiple methods, and collaboratively debating the magnitude of impact from the intervention.

Diagnosis and Discovery—using various assessment strategies to understand what each student brings to the lesson, including prior knowledge, motivations, and willingness to learn.

★ You are here.

Implementation—a deep knowledge and understanding of the practices required to implement anything well.

Intervention—having multiple interventions such that if one does not work with the student the teacher changes to another intervention. In addition to knowing high-probability interventions, it is knowing when to adapt and apply thoughtful design in planning for learning.

Following diagnosis and intervention comes implementation. Only when we have truly discovered our learners and their unique dispositions, and understood which interventions are likely to provide the best learning opportunities, can we truly be ready to implement these interventions with intention. Simply put, high-probability implementation of effective interventions has the potential to close learners' gaps in skill, will, and thrill. Both deep knowledge and understanding of learners and the specific interventions are required for high-impact implementation. Implementation may appear to be as simple as using the strategy within the context of a particular topic or lesson. For example, Fred

Murphy, an art teacher in a secondary school, wants his learners to understand the similarities and differences between Impressionism and Postimpressionism. "I recognize that this requires learners to apply their understanding of the elements of art, the characteristics of an individual time period, and then extract similarities and differences. They also have to synthesize this information into a coherent conclusion." Mr. Murphy decided to provide a Venn diagram to his learners, but allow them the choice of which piece of art in each time period would be the focus of their work. "The assignment was a disaster. They focused on irrelevant characteristics and never moved beyond superficial characteristics. At the end of the day, they did not know or understand the differences between these two closely aligned time periods in art history."

The frustration felt by Mr. Murphy is one that we can all relate to in our own teaching and learning. His initial assessments indicated that this was new learning; he recognized that asking learners to identify similarities and differences was a high-probability intervention. What happened? The answer is implementation. High-impact teachers like Mr. Murphy make decisions on a day-to-day basis that they believe will truly have an impact on their students. Great teaching by design is more than choosing an intervention that aligns to learners' needs and dropping it into a lesson plan. There are other factors we must take into account.

Our focus for this part of the DIIE model is to describe the process of implementation (see Figure 4.2). Educators cannot just rely on the potential of high-probability interventions, but must capitalize on this potential by designing the implementation to reflect the local context of the learning environment with its unique characteristics, learner dispositions, and learning experiences.

> Educators cannot just rely on the potential of high-probability interventions, but must capitalize on this potential by designing the implementation to reflect the local context of the learning environment with its unique characteristics, learner dispositions, and learning experiences.

Figure 4.2 The essential parts of implementing

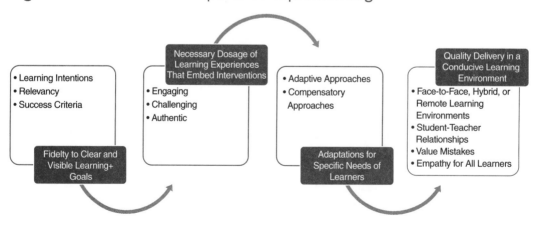

For Mr. Murphy, and all of us, successful implementation of high-probability interventions that maximize student learning requires us to think about our role as a teacher in a very distinct way. This thinking draws on the mindframes presented in Chapter 1 of this book. The ways in which educators think about their role in implementing instruction drives the decisions they make about each of the essential components of implementation. For example, if we believe that we are ready for the challenge of learning, and evaluators of our own impact on student learning, then we are more likely to design and implement a learning environment that welcomes mistakes and thus allows learners to engage in a productive learning struggle. Furthermore, we are more likely to design learning experiences that have the right level of challenge. As a final example, believing that all learners possess the capability to be successful and we are change agents moves us to provide the necessary adaptive and compensatory approaches to ensure students are moving toward explicit success criteria. Let's look at each essential part of implementation.

Fidelity to Clear and Visible Learning+® Goals

Providing clear and visible learning goals for learning is about us, teachers, identifying and sharing learning expectations with learners. These expectations are not limited to cognitive expectations, but also include behavioral and social-emotional expectations. In other words, we should share clear expectations related to the skill, will, and thrill of our learners. It is not enough for us to have clarity about learning from analyzing the standards, but we must engage our learners with these learning goals so that they can achieve the following (Frey, Hattie, & Fisher, 2018):

1. Know and describe their current level of knowledge, skills, and understanding.

2. Identify where they are going next in the learning journey and have the confidence to take on that challenge.

3. Select and utilize tools to move their learning forward.

4. See mistakes as learning opportunities, seeking feedback from their peers and us.

5. Monitor their own learning progress and make adjustments when necessary.

6. Recognize their own learning and support their peers in their own learning journey.

These six characteristics of assessment-capable visible learners represent the ideal blend of skill, will, and thrill.

As a result of clear and Visible Learning+ goals, learners should be able to answer these questions each and every day regarding their learning experience (Fisher, Frey, & Hattie, 2016, p. 21):

1. What am I learning today?

2. Why am I learning this?

3. How will I know that I learned it?

The first question requires that we have clear content, language, and social learning intentions that are visible to our learners so that they too are aware of today's learning. The "why" question helps us establish the authenticity of the learning so that we can place specific content, skills, and understandings within a relevant context. And, lastly, the third elicits a clear and concise description of what success looks like for both us and our learners.

Learning Intentions. Learning intentions establish what it is that our students are learning. Learning intentions are more than a standard; they are derived and based on the expectations articulated in national and state standards of learning. Simply writing an objective on the dry erase board and then reading it aloud waters down the power of a learning intention, which should focus the entire lesson and serve as an organizing feature of the learning students will engage in during the block or period. In this way, the learning intention drives the teaching and learning, supporting learners as they develop a better awareness of their progress toward expectations. Returning to Mr. Murphy's art history class, he developed the following learning intentions:

> *Content Learning Intention*: Today, I am learning about the similarities and differences between Impressionism and Postimpressionism art.
>
> *Language Learning Intention*: Today, I am learning the language necessary for communicating my aesthetic judgements.
>
> *Social Learning Intention*: Today, I am learning about constructive criticism and its role in making aesthetic judgements of others works of art.

From these learning intentions, Mr. Murphy is not just interested in content. He also looks at their language and interactions around the analysis of art—both his learners' works of art and works of art from the two time periods.

Success Criteria. Even with clear learning intentions, Mr. Murphy and his learners must have a clear picture of what success looks like. The success criteria describe how students will be expected to demonstrate their learning and can take many forms. Success criteria can be presented as "I can" statements, look-fors, rubrics, student work examples, models, or demonstrations. That's not to say that success criteria are just a culminating activity, but, instead, clear and concise statements of the evidence that learners will be asked to produce, showing where they are in their learning progression. Let's return to Mr. Murphy's learning intentions and consider the following ways that students will be expected to demonstrate success based on those learning intentions.

- I can describe elements of art and perspective techniques in pieces of art.
- I can identify major characteristics of Impressionism and Postimpressionism art.
- I can explain how art and culture reflect and influence each other.
- I can compare and contrast Impressionism with Postimpressionism art.
- I can justify my personal perception of an artist's intent, using visual clues and research.

Success criteria guide the implementation of high-probability interventions in three ways:

1. They provide the guardrails for learners as they become aware of the success criteria and engage with the criteria to move their learning forward.

2. The level of cognitive engagement, indicated by the verb, helps align the right intervention at the right time.

3. These criteria are the launch points for differentiating instruction to ensure all learners are moving toward the success criteria.

Student Awareness of Success Criteria

Similar to the pre-learning phase of a lesson, learners who are aware of what it means to be successful are able to engage in more goal-directed behavior. For example, if learners in Mr. Murphy's class are aware that they have to identify major characteristics, explain art and culture, or justify, they can better set goals for how they plan to leverage their current skills to meet those criteria. In addition, they can begin to monitor their current level of understanding and where they need to go next in their learning. In addition, when Mr. Murphy's learners are explicitly taught the success criteria, they

Figure 4.3 Example of a single-point rubric

Areas That Need Work	Success Criteria	Evidence of Exceeding Standards
	Topic introduced effectively.	
	Related ideas grouped together to give some organization.	
	Topic developed with multiple facts, definitions, details.	
	Linking words and phrases connect ideas within a category of information.	
	Strong concluding statement or section.	
5th Grade Writing Rubric		

Source: Nancy Frey.

can select learning strategies that will move their learning forward, provided they have also been explicitly taught those learning strategies.

One specific example of sharing success criteria with students is the single-point rubric, shown in Figure 4.3.

Mrs. Wood uses a single-point writing rubric with her fifth graders to explicitly share success criteria in a way that promotes ownership of their own learning. Single-point rubrics, when explicitly taught to learners, provide the guardrails for students to self-assess and then use metacognitive strategies to engage in self-directed learning. In the end, this increases the probability of successfully moving toward the explicit success criteria and increasing their will (dispositions) and thrill (motivations).

Data from our many learning walks indicate that learners are very good at stating what it is they are learning (i.e., the learning intention), but often struggle describing how they know when they are successful. Success criteria can be used to engage learners in planning and prediction, student-generated goal setting, co-constructing the criteria, or using an advanced organizer.

Success Criteria and Aligning the Intervention

As we have pointed out before, to actualize the potential of a high-probability intervention, that intervention must be used at the right time. Success criteria are linked to actions and allow the learner to make their learning visible. Thus, the way Mr. Murphy's learners demonstrate their learning should align with the expectations. Consider the success criteria, "I can describe elements of art and perspective techniques in pieces of art." The action in this statement is *describe*. If that is how learners are expected to demonstrate their learning, they must learn and use learning strategies that give them opportunities to describe. Thus, Mr. Murphy and his learners might capitalize on high-probability interventions like summarizing, think-pair-share, or student discussion. Each of these interventions engage learners in *describing*. If Mr. Murphy had decided to use response clickers and a series of multiple-choice questions, learners might enjoy the intervention, but they would be identifying rather than describing. This would be misaligned with the success criteria and may not move learners toward the expectations for the day. As we all know, the act of identifying something is very different from describing something. What if Mr. Murphy had created and implemented a sorting task where learners sorted a collection of characteristics into two piles: Impressionism and Postimpressionism. Again, sorting expects learners to recognize. However, this is very different from the explicit success criteria that expects learners to compare and contrast Impressionism with Postimpressionism art.

Necessary Dosage of an Engaging, Challenging, and Authentic Learning Experience

Providing learners with an engaging experience or authentic task provides a relevant context for their learning, allowing them to answer the question "why am I learning this?" Mr. Murphy's learners were tasked with learning about two very similar time periods in art history. This may not be interesting or engaging to everyone in his class. The nature of the task evokes a level of engagement that either makes each learner's thinking visible or disengages students. There has been considerable work on what improves a learner's perception of task value. Eccles (2005) believes that subjective task value is a function of four components:

1. *Interest*: the enjoyment one gets from engaging in the task.

2. *Utility value*: the instrumental value of the task or activity for helping to fulfill another short- or long-range goal.

3. *Attainment value*: the link between the task and one's sense of self and either personal or social identity.

4. *Cost:* what may be given up by making a specific choice or the negative experiences associated with each possible choice.

The application of this research suggests that learners persist in engaging in an experience or task when the task meets the following criteria: has clear and modeled expectations, is emotionally safe for learners to take academic risks, allows them to personalize their response, provides opportunities for choice and social interaction, and presents a novel and authentic way of seeing the content (see Antonetti & Stice, 2018).

The actions articulated in the success criteria support both teachers and learners as they select high-probability learning tools that align with the expectations and the level of cognitive engagement. This moves us beyond the examples of interventions shared in the previous chapters to the broader database of high-probability interventions. Timing matters for all of these interventions and the criteria for success should inform that timing.

> The actions articulated in the success criteria support both teachers and learners as they select high-probability learning tools that align with the expectations and the level of cognitive engagement.

Adaptations Through Adaptive and Compensatory Approaches

So, how do we get all learners to move toward the explicit success criteria when they enter our learning environment with such diverse characteristics, dispositions, and prior knowledge? This is what differentiated instruction has long sought to address. But the question remains: how to differentiate in the era of accountability. The use of adaptive and compensatory approaches based on high expectations (i.e., learning intentions and success criteria) for all learners helps to answer that question. By compensatory supports, we mean additional supports designed to leverage learners' strengths and at the same time address skill gaps that may impede their ability to move forward in their learning. With compensatory approaches, the essential learning is held constant, and the means for acquiring and consolidating that learning is differentiated to meet the needs of students.

Some learners require additional adaptive supports that serve to accommodate or modify learning expectations. Accommodations don't substantially change the learning outcomes for students, but instead are designed to improve access to those opportunities. Accommodations can include changes to testing and assessment materials, access to assistive and adaptive technology, adaptations in the physical environment or in how information is presented, and alterations to timing and scheduling for the benefit of the learner. On the other hand, modifications are more significant adaptations and involve decisions that alter the learning expectations for students. Modifications are reserved for students with more significant disabilities. The majority of students with disabilities receive accommodations; comparatively few receive modifications. Therefore, accommodations are about "the how"—how a student receives knowledge and demonstrates mastery. Modifications are about "the what"—what knowledge a student is responsible for learning, and what knowledge he or she will not be learning at this time (Fisher & Frey, 2004).

Success criteria provide the starting point for differentiating instruction to ensure all learners have equitable access and opportunity for moving toward success. The specific learning experiences or tasks that rely on high-probability interventions can provide equitable access and opportunity to learn. Mr. Murphy wants to ensure that every student has the opportunity to succeed in his or her learning about Impressionism and Postimpressionism. Similarly, another teacher, Mrs. Wood wants all of her learners to succeed as writers. To provide the necessary compensatory or adaptive approaches based on who our learners are, we have to look at the success criteria and learning experiences through lenses of difficulty and complexity.

Complexity describes the level of thinking required to engage in the learning experience and accomplish the task. For example, to identify is less cognitively complex than comparing and contrasting. Similarly, analyzing represents greater cognitive complexity than describing. Difficulty, then, describes the amount of effort required to engage in the learning experience, accomplish the task, and meet the criteria for success. Responding to 25 questions about a text passage contains a greater degree of difficulty than responding to one or two questions about the author's use of symbolism in Chapter 2 of a text. Likewise, working one multistep mathematics problem is less difficult than working 30 mathematics problems, saying nothing about the complexity of the task. In the end, anything our learners do related to content, skills, and understanding can be described in terms of both complexity and difficulty. For example, some experiences may be of high complexity, but low difficulty to promote metacognition. Others may be of low complexity, but high difficulty to encourage persistence. But more to our point, this is where differentiation comes into play.

The success criteria articulate the expectations for all learners. They set the level of complexity, or cognitive engagement, expected of all learners. Thus, to ensure equity of access and opportunity, we should hold complexity constant. If Mr. Murphy expects his learners to compare and contrast, all learners should engage in comparing and contrasting regardless of their unique characteristics, dispositions, or gaps in skill. While holding complexity constant, we then adjust the level of difficulty by using compensatory and adaptive approaches. Let's look at a specific example using Mr. Murphy's success criteria. Mr. Murphy has indicated the level of complexity through the verbs in his success criteria: *describe, identify, explain, compare and contrast,* and *justify.* "I know that some of my learners will need support during today's learning. I have some learners that struggle in their reading, several of my learners are learning English as their second language, and there are two individuals with a physical disability."

Mr. Murphy will have to adjust the difficulty of the learning experience or task without wavering on the level of complexity. How can he adjust the difficulty of the learning to ensure each of the students he wants to support can move toward the success criteria? "For my students that have reading challenges, I provide different resources related to Impressionism and Postimpressionism. For example, I provide different text sets with different Lexile scores, I provide audio-visual clips, and I often provide skeleton notes for them to organize their thinking." Mr. Murphy has adjusted the difficulty caused by reading so that these students could engage in the new learning at the highest level of complexity.

"I offer learners different ways of identifying, describing, explaining, comparing and contrasting, and justifying. They might do this verbally, in writing, on a computer, with a peer, or through the use of a graphic organizer or concept map." Adjusting for difficulty while maintaining complexity does not get in the way of a learner justifying an analysis of Impressionist and Postimpressionist paintings. Students can demonstrate the expected level of complexity through assistive and adaptive technology or adaptations to what information they access and how they access information.

In the end, the implementation of any high-probability intervention (e.g., student discussion, reciprocal teaching, jigsaw, vocabulary programs, deliberate practice, etc.) requires that educators consider compensatory and adaptive approaches to differentiate the difficulty of the task while maintaining the complexity of the learning. This leads us into the final part of implementation which requires creating an environment for successful implementation.

Quality Delivery in an Environment for Implementation

An environment for implementation has never been more important as schools and classrooms engage in implementing of what works best in remote learning environments as either the only mode for teaching and learning, or hybrid with face-to-face teaching and learning. In each of these scenarios, quality delivery must take into account the social-emotional aspects and the physical aspects of the learning environment. Ensuring that implementation is successful, whether in the science laboratory or the living room—at classroom desks or on the couch—requires us to keep our focus on the intervention that works best and then leverage available resources to move from potential to implementation.

Social-Emotional Aspects. To ignore the social-emotional aspect of implementation in any environment would overlook some of the strongest factors associated with student learning. In both face-to-face and virtual environments, class cohesion, teacher credibility, feeling a part of the learning community, and learner's self-efficacy, require educators recognize the unique dispositions students bring to class and create an inclusive environment that enhances their will and thrill for learning. Whether or not a learner goes along with the interventions we seek to implement in any learning environment is a product of our relationships with our learners and the learning environment we design.

> Whether or not a learner goes along with the interventions we seek to implement in our any learning environment is a product of our relationships with our learners and the learning environment we design.

Teacher-Student Relationships. Teacher-student relationships have an average effect size of 0.48, suggesting that this factor has a positive influence on student growth and achievement. Teacher-student relationships also have implications on our ability to truly get to know our learners and make the class a safe place to learn, make mistakes, and learn from errors. Beyond using online learning platforms as a means for delivering content, we have to capitalize on interactive features (e.g., chat rooms, breakout rooms, etc. . . .) to engage with learners around social-emotional aspects of their learning. A "morning meeting" can and should be a part of our virtual learning environments just as this time has become essential in brick and mortar classrooms. Social interaction with peers and teachers is essential in building relationships from afar. After all, if a learner does not have a good relationship with his or her teacher, the learner may be more likely to, say, hide mistakes and errors or take less risks in engaging in experiences or tasks. Without knowing our learners, we are less likely to identify and implement an intervention that moves learning forward for that student.

Take for example, teacher clarity. Although clarity for learning requires us to be deliberate, intentional, and purposeful in the what, why, and how of learning, a key factor in students engaging in that learning is the teacher-student relationship. Teacher-student relationships should foster, nurture, and sustain a learning culture that sees mistakes and errors as learning opportunities; these in turn encourage teachers and learners to give and receive feedback. Again, this cannot occur without strong, positive teacher-student relationships.

As each of us recalls our favorite teacher, think about an individual that you believe had the greatest impact on your cognitive, behavioral, and social-emotional growth? What specific qualities did that teacher have? Cornelius-White's (2007) meta-analysis on student-centered teaching revealed critical attributes of teachers who fostered, nurtured, and sustained strong, positive relationships with their students. The attributes of warmth, trust, and empathy lead to positive relationships:

- *Warmth*: Warmth is demonstrated in acceptance, affection, unconditional respect, and positive regard for students. Teachers must show warmth in observable ways rather than simply intend to do so.

- *Trust*: Trust occurs when students see that the teacher believes in them—especially when they struggle. Teachers need to have the expectation that students will be successful and that what teachers want them to learn is worth learning.

- *Empathy*: Teachers need to take the perspective of students if they are to get through to them. When this is understood, a teacher can know the optimal feedback to provide to move the student forward.

These attributes are the essence of positive relationships, that is "the student seeing the warmth, feeling the encouragement and the teacher's high expectations, and knowing that the teacher understands him or her" (Hattie, 2012, p. 158). As Mr. Murphy points out, "I love my students and they know it. They know that mistakes help us learn, that I want them to try things out, and that I want them to let me know when they need help. This takes effort on my part, but it all starts with trust. They trust that I am not going to embarrass them, single them out, or leave them to fend for themselves. Now, I am not gonna make it easy on them, but they know I will be right there beside them when they struggle."
Mr. Murphy points out that in many cases we must develop the attributes of positive teacher-student relationships. As with all other aspects of teaching, these skills develop and grow as we apply our evaluative thinking skills. In this specific instance, how can we engage with our students across both face-to-face and virtual contexts in a strong and positive way to truly understand who they are as learners?

Establishing and leveraging teacher-student relationships is challenging in any environment. With the added variable of remote learning, there is added complexity and difficulty to these relationships. The complexity of these relationships comes from the developmental aspect of working with young learners, from age 5 to 18. The difficulty of these relationships comes from the establishment of boundaries (e.g., being "friendly" with students). For example, teachers must be warm while maintaining their professional standards. "You have to go much deeper than that and actually start to engage with students around their curiosity, their interests, and their habits of mind through understanding and approaching material to really be an effective teacher" (Sparks, 2019). In remote learning environments, we can easily slip into a less formal exchange, forgetting that norms and expectations for appropriate interactions on the computer are just as important as face-to-face norms and expectations.

To ensure successful implementation, educators must also consider the unique cultural dispositions through an environment of empathy. The challenge for teachers is to create an environment where all students can feel welcome regardless of where they are in their learning journey. Once again, establishing norms for all interactions sets the tone that this is a safe place for learning. In addition to strong, positive teacher-student relationships, the simplest and most impactful disposition a teacher can foster is empathy. Being empathetic (seeing learning through the eyes of the student) can promote opportunities for learning that extend beyond the curriculum. Empathy from a teaching perspective is how positive teacher-student relationships will flourish. Empathy promotes opportunities for teachers to learn about the culture of their students, and in turn students to learn about each other's culture. Beyond the obvious positive social-emotional learning attributes, empathy allows us to understand our learners' perspectives and use that to better implement authentic, high-probability interventions. Knowing more about our students' backgrounds, and the special knowledge they bring to our classes, will allow us to purposefully, intentionally, and deliberately further develop their skill, will, and thrill.

For example, teachers across Canada have fostered and nurtured environments of reconciliation through creating environments of empathy. After the release of UNDRIP (United Nations Declaration on the Rights of Indigenous Peoples), the Truth and Reconciliation Commission of Canada (2008–2015) outlined a plan with the intention that Canadians become more educated in the truth of the treatment of Indigenous peoples throughout Canadian history. The commission, now known as the National Centre for Truth and Reconciliation, actively promotes professional learning that engages teachers in learning about Indigenous culture, and strategies to explore Indigenous ways of knowing. By actively engaging in professional learning experiences, teachers model cultural empathy for their students. This attitude is then fostered with students, ensuring all are feeling safe and comfortable in their classes. Using staff professional learning time to create opportunities to learn about the cultures that exist within the school can pay dividends as we engage in learning with our students. In learning about specific cultural dispositions and nuances, we can then implement strategies and construct lessons that have a truer sense of personalization for students.

At the beginning of each new semester, high school social studies teacher Mr. Spilak takes time to learn about the various cultural backgrounds of his students. His background he has designed for his remote learning platform contains flags from around the world, to represent the variety of cultural backgrounds that have passed through his classroom. "I find that by taking time to learn more about the students who are in my class, I can immediately foster a connection with them." He notes that by leaning on his culture as a means to spark conversations, students can see aspects of themselves in him as a teacher. By understanding and celebrating the variety of student backgrounds that cross paths in his social studies class, Mr. Spilak ensures that the students themselves become the focal point of his social studies lessons about globalization and ideology. Here is the clear message: If Mr. Spilak had not fostered and nurtured this type of learning environment, any high-probability intervention might never have moved beyond a hypothetical effect size. By attending to the will and thrill of his learners, implementing learning experiences and tasks becomes a genuine and authentic collaboration between the teacher and students. "My students log-on ready to learn about new concepts in social studies because they are excited to infuse their prior knowledge and experiences in the new learning activities. We used Google Docs and breakout rooms to establish norms for how we collaborate with each other." Students have noted that Mr. Spilak's care to include all students in learning by using their own background knowledge creates an environment that they really want to be a part of—a feat that is sometimes very difficult to do with high school students.

Physical Environment. Successful implementation is a matter of purposeful design. And one often-neglected design element is the physical environment in which students learn. If you and your learners are working in a face-to-face, brick and mortar classroom, there are decisions we can make that can have a great influence on learning. This notion is supported by the Australian Children's Education & Care Quality Authority (2018) as they recognize: "The physical environment is never simply a backdrop to the curriculum; it is an integral part of the curriculum or leisure-based program. An environment with rich and built-in learning opportunities also frees educators to interact with children." The physical environment can foster or hinder the effective implementation of any learning tool or intervention. The way classrooms are designed and arranged should reflect the ways in which strategies and interventions will be implemented. Likewise, the way our remote learning environments are set up should reflect the ways in which strategies and interventions will be implemented.

In face-to-face environments, the physical arrangement of the classroom is often driven by other factors outside of the curriculum. Let's say that a teacher wants to use the jigsaw method. With an effect size of 1.20, this intervention has the potential to accelerate student learning. Of course, the selection of that intervention should be based on what the students need to learn (the diagnosis or discovery phase). But the implementation of a jigsaw requires that the classroom layout be conducive to success. Placing students in rows with physical barriers between them will not promote the deep consolidation of learning that the jigsaw method can yield. Teachers have the power to make deliberate choices with respect to the physical environment that can enhance, rather than stall, the implementation process. To take excerpts from Malaguzzi (1984), "We value space, to create a handsome environment and its potential to inspire social, affective, and cognitive learning. The space is an aquarium that mirrors the ideas and values of the people who live in it" (p. 339). Malaguzzi termed the physical environment the "third teacher," following the adult and the peers as the first and second teachers. We believe the consideration of the physical environment is just as important as the consideration of empathy and teacher-student relationships for implementing effective teaching.

For example, Vicente Margulies, a high school social studies teacher, tries to make optimal use of the physical environment in his 12th-grade (senior) class. His entire course is focused around the concept of ideology, and as such, students are required to understand the ideological spectrum as a measurement tool to place key historical figures according to their beliefs. In one lesson, Mr. Margulies organized his seating arrangement according to the beliefs and ideologies of his students. It started with a direct lesson on what an ideological spectrum was, including the difference between right-wing and left-wing politics. Making it very clear that individuals can have beliefs that vary according to issue, the students sat themselves according to where they thought they would be on the spectrum. As the semester progressed, students were moved (and moved themselves) when they found their beliefs would shift according to issue. The most prominent example was with one of his students who started the year as a left-wing economic supporter, but ended on the right-wing. When asked about his move, the student reported that he found himself agreeing with more capitalist economic beliefs. Over the course of the year, thanks to the design of the physical environment, students were continually self-assessing their ideology according to issues that were raised in class. The physical environment provided the medium in which the students could experience the impact of ideological measurement in real time. In this example specifically, the physical space was purposefully designed for implementation.

There are many considerations for the physical environment. For example, harsh lights and loud noises such as chairs scraping across the floor can interfere with students' concentration. If furniture blocks a teachers' ability to move easily around the room, some students are less likely to have individual interactions with that teacher and might not have their errors noticed. If there is a classroom library, for example, the dedication of that space communicates to students that reading is important and that there are places to go to find things to read. The walls also contribute to students' learning. In some classes, the walls are plain, void of anything, which might contribute to boredom. In other classrooms, the walls are so busy that they are a source of distraction. There is no one right way to arrange the physical environment but there are some general guidelines that teachers can consider:

- Make the space work for the planned interventions. If students need to discuss with peers, ensure the environment allows for that. If students need lab space, plan for it. If students need quiet, individual workspaces, arrange for that.

- Reduce the "teacher only" space and dedicate more of the learning environment to the tasks and activities that foster learning.

- Consider the walls as part of the learning environment. They should not be distracting, but they can be used as a resource. For example, a word wall that is used for teaching vocabulary might be useful whereas faded motivational posters may not be.

- Be aware of some students' need to see an exit. Don't block the exit, visually or physically, as it can be threatening to students, especially those who have experienced trauma.

- Generally, avoid neon bright colors, as they can cause tension and heighten anxiety. Pastels, neutral colors, and earth tones are usually better.

- Monitor areas or actions that cause loud noises and try to minimize the impact of the noise.

As with instructional tools and teaching in general, there is no one right way to ensure that the environment facilitates learning. Our point here is to ensure that the physical environment is conducive to the implementation of the selected instructional interventions. Thus far, we have focused on the physical environment but online, distance, and blended learning environments also can either facilitate or hinder learning. When students enter a virtual learning space, they should feel comfortable. They should be greeted. The site should be predicable. And the learning expectations should be clear. Each "room" that they enter should convey the ways in which learning will occur. Many of the same guidelines that we have addressed in this chapter apply to virtual and distance learning. Bright colors and loud noises are probably not a good idea. Clear directions for a task are a better idea. As you plan for distance or distributed learning, consider the experience and what that experience is communicating to students. Table 4.1 contains some ideas to hack a classroom or remote learning space. In the case of a remote learning space, we must work collaboratively with our learners to help them set up the best physical environment for their own learning. This will also allow us to build on a positive teacher–student relationship, encouraging students to self-reflect, self-monitor, and self-evaluate their own learning environments. A great way to build warmth, trust, and empathy is to talk to learners about how to set up their remote learning environment.

Table 4.1 Hack your space

Purpose	Hack
Improve movement.	Face-to-face: Retrofit wheels on old tables. Remote: Encourage learners to find a space where they can stand in front of the computer and move around; we should model this by incorporating movement in our learning experiences.
Reduce noise.	Face-to-face: Add tennis balls to chair legs. Remote: Brainstorm with learners about locations in their learning space that will be as noise free as possible; when teaching, eliminate as much noise as possible on your end and use a high-quality microphone.
Improve lighting.	Face-to-face: Add a dimmer switch and small lamps to warm up the environment. Remote: Suggest that learners adjust the shades or add lighting if possible; for the teacher, we should make sure our lighting allows learners to see us and what we are sharing on our screens.
Improve visual interest.	Face-to-face: Add positive messages and reduce clutter by organizing materials. Remote: For the teacher, ensure the use of high-quality visuals and reduce the amount of text on the screen.
Bring nature into the classroom.	Face-to-face: Add a plant, a water feature, pictures of beautiful vistas, and images of nature (e.g., animals, weather, flowers). Remote: For teachers, use concrete examples or objects from around the house that represent who we are (e.g., picture of our family, our pets, or objects related to the days lesson).
Develop a sheltered place.	Face-to-face: Use an upholstered chair or bean bag chair and fill the space with objects for students to hold, such as a pillow or other soft object. Remote: Provide learners with ways to communicate that they need to step away from the computer; explicitly teach strategies and develop a plan for going to a space other than in front of the computer.

Fostering an Environment of Mistakes

As we noted in Chapter 1, the decisions educators make in establishing learning environments are driven by specific mindframes. An environment that allows for mistakes and errors is consistent with the ninth mindframe: *I build relationships and trust so that learning can occur in a place where it is safe to make mistakes and learn from others.* This mindframe is absolutely paramount in the creation of strong, positive teacher-student relationships that allow for teachers to know their learners, their learners' dispositions, unique characteristics, and where they have learning opportunities. These relationships form the foundation on which we foster an environment in which mistakes and errors are not seen as deficits, but opportunities for learning. We acknowledge that this is easier said than done. A learners' expectations or prior concepts about what it means to be a learner and to be a "good student" can be a barrier to their seeing mistakes and errors as valuable to their learning. One of the most humbling, but self-reflective tasks we can do as teachers is to interview our learners now and throughout the school year. Putting our evaluative thinking caps on, simply ask your students, what is a good learner in this learning environment?

Far too many students believe that a "good student" knows the answer, sits quietly, completes assigned tasks, and arrives (or logs in) on time. In fact, these were the most common responses from a survey of over 800 students. One of our priorities must be to disrupt students' notion of a "good student." In part, we hope students come to understand that good students learn from their mistakes. Boaler (2016), through her work on mathematical mindsets, suggests the following three strategies to encourage the celebration of mistakes in the learning environment:

1. Foster the love of mistakes by talking openly about the reason they are important for learning. Not only will this bring out other learners' perspectives, but these moments are now available for all students as opportunities to learn.

2. Don't just praise mistakes but talk about why they are important for learning. One example of this strategy is the explicit teaching of how mistakes and errors promote better learning based on how our brains encode information.

3. Finally, provide learners with experiences and tasks that allow for different approaches and perspectives. This actually opens the door to more mistakes and makes this part of the way "we do business in this class."

Leah Acala is a middle school mathematics teacher who has found a way to integrate these three strategies into her teaching. She uses a technique called "My Favorite No." In this activity, she presents a problem to her learners that can be solved by more than one approach. Her learners independently solve the problem without putting their name on the index card she provided for them. Ms. Acala moves around the room to gauge the pace of her learners as they tackle the problem. She asks herself: Who needs more time? Who is struggling? Who seems to have a high level of proficiency with this type of problem?

QR Code 4.1 Developing an Environment of Mistakes: My Favorite No Activity (Acala, 2018)

After some time, Ms. Acala stops her learners and provides the "final answer" to the problem. She then asks her learners to come sit on the floor in the front of the room where they then place their index cards into one of three piles: "Yes, Correct and Confident," "Yes, Correct, But Unsure," and "No, Need Some Feedback."

To maintain an environment in which mistakes and errors are valued, Ms. Acala chooses a response from the "No, Need Some Feedback" pile, which she explains is a response that was incorrect but had elements of the response that were "on the right track." She then takes measures to rewrite the student response on a new index card under a document camera. From there, she engages her learners in a discussion surrounding what the student did that was mathematically correct. After a few minutes, she prompts the class to make suggestions about where to go next with the selected response. When discussing the process of "My Favorite No," Ms. Acala notes how this activity allows for all students to thrive in the midst of mistakes. As she says, "All of my students are very engaged. They feel like they're not getting penalized for being wrong, and they feel supported by their peers. In fact, they often ask for their own 'No, Need Some Feedback' to be selected for discussion."

Samantha, a student in Ms. Acala's class says, "I like my 'No' to be picked. I know that I made a mistake and really want to figure out what I could do next time." Ms. Acala follows up with, "It's very comforting to hear them ask and then expect to get feedback. When we do this on a regular basis and I can hear their thinking, I am no longer surprised by what they don't know. They're not surprised by what they don't know. It's how it should be. It creates more of a dialogue about what we need to do to address their learning needs."

This same activity can be done in a remote learning environment using Google Docs and taking a poll (e.g., Mentimeter).

Of course, implementation is more than just picking interventions that have a high effect size and then dropping them into a lesson plan. Implementation is not simply the third, discrete step in the DIIE model. At this point, you likely see the interconnectedness of each component of the model. The diagnosis and discovery of where learners are was presented first. That led to the identification and consideration of interventions, with some selected based on students' needs relative to their skill, will, and thrill. Implementation demands that we take each high-probability intervention and adapt that intervention to reflect the context of our own learning environment. In many ways, implementation requires teachers to make deliberate and precise choices that will lead to seamless implementation. We do this with the following:

- Translating our standards-based expectations into clear learning intentions and success criteria: These should be in student-friendly language that engage students in their own learning.

- Using the success criteria as guardrails to design experiences or tasks that embed the high-probability interventions into the learning: For example, reciprocal teaching is not learning. Reciprocal teaching is the intervention by which we help our learners deepen their learning around content and understandings through summarizing, questioning, clarifying, and predicting. The intervention is the tool.

- Differentiating learning experiences or tasks to ensure equity of access and opportunity for all learners: This involves differentiating the difficulty through compensatory and adaptive approaches while maintaining the level of complexity. This ensures all learners are progressing toward explicit success criteria.

- Creating an environment that promotes implementation through strong, positive student-teacher relationships: This is built on warmth, trust, and empathy. The physical environment should also be considered. Learners must feel like they are valued members of the learning community. This begins with us!

The next component of the DIIE model focuses on impact. Assuming that the diagnosis was correct, the intervention was appropriate, and the implementation was successful, impact should be assured. But, we cannot leave that to chance. Great teaching by design requires that we ask the question: Did I have an impact on students' learning? Let's turn our attention to evaluating our impact.

"
Evaluation is not an end, but the starting point for making decisions about where to go next.

5

CHAPTER 5

EVALUATION

Figure 5.1 The DIIE model

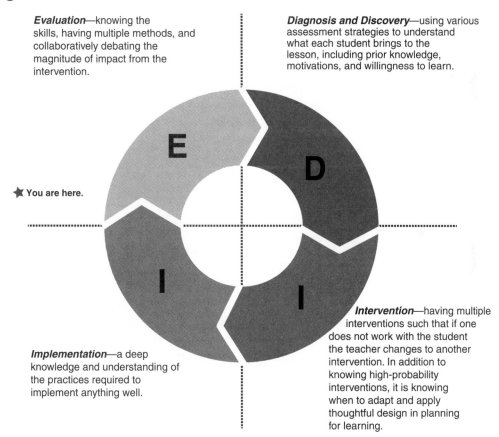

Evaluation—knowing the skills, having multiple methods, and collaboratively debating the magnitude of impact from the intervention.

Diagnosis and Discovery—using various assessment strategies to understand what each student brings to the lesson, including prior knowledge, motivations, and willingness to learn.

★ You are here.

Intervention—having multiple interventions such that if one does not work with the student the teacher changes to another intervention. In addition to knowing high-probability interventions, it is knowing when to adapt and apply thoughtful design in planning for learning.

Implementation—a deep knowledge and understanding of the practices required to implement anything well.

The final component of the DIIE model, and thus great teaching by design, is *evaluation*. Evaluation requires knowing about, and using, specific skills to determine our impact on student learning. And good evaluations draw on multiple methods of assessment both during the learning and after the learning. After *we implement what works best*, we must use robust evidence generated by our learners to know with confidence, *did my implementation of what works best result in student learning?*

Figure 5.2 Essential parts of evaluating

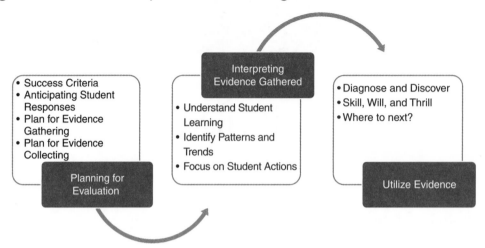

- Success Criteria
- Anticipating Student Responses
- Plan for Evidence Gathering
- Plan for Evidence Collecting

Planning for Evaluation

Interpreting Evidence Gathered

- Understand Student Learning
- Identify Patterns and Trends
- Focus on Student Actions

- Diagnose and Discover
- Skill, Will, and Thrill
- Where to next?

Utilize Evidence

> Evaluation allows us to define the magnitude of the impact our intervention had on our students, and with that information we can determine where to go next in the learning progression.

Implementation without gathering evidence of learning and then evaluating that evidence to determine our impact leaves teaching and learning to chance. Evaluation allows us to define the magnitude of impact our intervention had on our students, and with that information we can determine where to go next in the learning progression. This step in the DIIE model involves the planning for evaluation, understanding the evidence gathered during implementation, and using that evidence to decide where to go next in teaching and learning (see Figure 5.2).

Ms. Harouff is an eighth-grade mathematics teacher who regularly reflects on her decisions about teaching. She works to strike the ideal balance between conceptual understanding, procedural knowledge, and the transfer of concepts and thinking to novel problems. "This can be quite a challenge, but worth it. I have to monitor students' thinking about mathematics concepts so that they do not develop misconceptions about certain procedures like the order of operations. Then, I want to make sure they appropriately apply their thinking, again to avoid misconceptions. I frequently engage in dialogue with my learners to get them to clarify their thinking. I often talk about learners' thinking with my colleagues. They can often give me insight into how learners are thinking about math."

Ms. Harouff uses the term "monitor" when talking about her role in supporting the learners in her class. In other words, her way of thinking about evaluation suggests that this is a continuous process, regularly providing her insight into her students' thinking. "As students are working or talking about ideas, I am always watching and listening to decide what they might need next to move forward in their learning. I also want them to use their own evidence and make adjustments to their learning." She has a broader view of evaluation, one that moves beyond an end-of-unit assessment or exam. Evaluation is not an end, but the starting point for making decisions about where to go next.

A Broader View of Evaluation

As teachers, we must balance the complexities associated with teaching and learning. For example, Ms. Harouff must manage the logistics of the learning environment (e.g., attendance, access to the Internet, materials, and supplies) along with responding to unplanned needs of her learners and colleagues (e.g., requests to see the nurse, interruptions over the intercom). These tasks are in addition to diagnosing, intervening, and implementing what works best. Evaluating our impact is hard. However, if we broaden our view of evaluation beyond a single assessment, one that requires that we delay our knowledge about impact until the end of the week, unit, or semester, we can infuse evaluation into every part of our teaching and learning. In other words, evaluation becomes a natural part of what we do in our learning environments. To know our impact, we have to utilize assessments *as* learning, *for* learning, and *of* learning.

Each learning experience or task offers us the opportunity to gain insight into student thinking and learning. Consider two of the high-probability interventions from Chapter 3, summarization (0.74 effect size) and elaborate interrogation (0.56 effect size). These two interventions have a dual purpose. First, they both have the potential to accelerate learning by allowing students to monitor and think critically about their own understanding. Second, when our learners summarize and respond to the "why" questions, their thinking becomes visible and available for us to evaluate. This is assessment *as* learning for the student and assessment *for* learning for us. In this case, the evaluation of impact was embedded in the teaching and learning of the day, not a separate, set aside time for a quiz, test, or exam. Although there is a place for these assessments *of* learning, they are limited in their ability to inform the just-in-time decisions teachers make during instruction. We will close out this chapter with a closer look at assessments *of* learning. First let's start with the *as* and *for* learning.

Using different ways of assessing compels us to break away from the idea that evaluation is linear: teach then test, teach then test, and so on. Learning is more fluid. This is especially true in developing learning environments that foster the *skill, will,* and *thrill* of learning. Recall that developing skill, will, and thrill is not a linear process either. If the development of skill, will, and thrill is fluid, then our assessment *as, for,* and *of* that learning must reflect that fluid nature as well. There will be times when our assessment

> Evaluation is not an end, but the starting point for making decisions about where to go next.

focuses more on skill development and other times when we focus on will, and that is okay. Yet it should be noted that all three need to be developed in balance, with our focus being on the process of learning and not just the product of learning. Furthermore, evaluation is not done in isolation, but through collaborative conversations between us, our colleagues, and our learners.

For educators to evaluate the impact of their implementation and make decisions based on that impact, they must make evaluation a continuous and embedded part of both teaching and learning.

> For educators to evaluate the impact of their implementation and make decisions based on that impact, they must make evaluation a continuous and embedded part of both teaching and learning.

Planning for Evaluation

Good evaluations start with a plan for evaluation. This planning involves revisiting previous components of the DIIE model. Planning for evaluation requires us to have clarity about our expectation of student success, a system to gather evidence of learning, and information about common errors and misconceptions using our prior experiences with the content and teaching.

Success Criteria and Evaluation. Success criteria articulate what evidence learners must produce to demonstrate their progress toward learning intentions (Ainsworth & Donovan, 2019). In addition to success criteria providing guardrails for aligning our choice of interventions and supporting more goal-directed behavior in our learners, these powerful statements guide educators in developing assessments *as* and *for* learning. Consider the following criteria for success from Ms. Fitzgerald's chemistry class.

- I can explain the process for balancing equations.

- I can predict products for different chemical reactions.

- I can justify my prediction.

- I can compare and contrast products for synthesis, decomposition, single-replacement, double-replacement, and combustion reactions.

The verb in each of these statements makes it clear how learners can demonstrate their learning. They also guide the evidence collection that allows us to evaluate our impact. The assessments would need to provide students' opportunities to explain, predict, justify, and compare and contrast. When planning for evaluation, the first place we look is the criteria for success that have been explicitly shared with our learners. Ms. Fitzgerald uses "I can" statements, but the same applies to look-fors, rubrics, student work examples, models, and demonstrations. Are learners able to demonstrate the look-fors, align their work with the exemplars and models, and transfer learning from the demonstrations? From here, we take these criteria and deliberately plan the development of assessments *as* and *for* learning.

Planning to Gather Evidence. When planning to evaluate impact, checks for understanding provide opportunities to gather evidence. Checking for understanding is a systematic approach used to monitor and adjust teaching based on student responses. An essential characteristic of evaluation is the teacher and the student actively and continuously monitoring student learning using specific strategies designed to gather evidence. These checks for understanding can range in complexity, intensity, and the means by which learners make their thinking visible. For example, checks for understanding can be written, verbal, or kinesthetic, depending on the criteria for success. The more directly and quickly we can obtain the necessary evidence, the better.

Returning to Ms. Fitzgerald's class, she and her colleagues have developed a plan to gather evidence that aligns with the "I can" statements. As she said, "We really spent time thinking about how we wanted to evaluate our learners' understanding during the lesson. We made this a central part of our planning conversation." Table 5.1 illustrates how this planning may look.

Ms. Fitzgerald and her colleagues have multiple methods of gathering evidence about students' learning. Furthermore,

> An essential characteristic of evaluation is the teacher and the student actively and continuously monitoring student learning using specific strategies designed to gather evidence.

Table 5.1   Example of an evidence-gathering plan

Criteria for Success	Activities to Gather Evidence
I can **explain** the process for balancing equations.	With partners, learners draw slips of paper from a ziplock baggie of equations provided to each pair of students; partners take turns explaining how to balance the equations, providing feedback and help to each other.
I can **predict** products for different chemical reactions.	Various activities include: think-pair-share using demonstrations of each reaction; student questioning during direct instruction using worked examples; guided practice with examples from textbook; exit ticket using clickers.
I can **justify** my prediction.	After a 1-minute write, learners turn to a neighbor and talk about what they think the product is.
I can **compare and contrast** products for synthesis, decomposition, single-replacement, double-replacement, and combustion reactions.	Various activities include: looking at contrasting cases to identify essential characteristics during direct instruction; independently sorting different reactions and then writing out reasons for sorting categories; a jigsaw to identify the essential characteristics of each type of reaction, and developing a concept map.

Source: Adapted from Sweeney, D., & Harris, L. S. (2016). *Student-centered coaching: The moves.* Thousand Oaks, CA: Corwin.

these assessments allow her to imbed evaluation into the very interventions she has decided to implement. "I want to monitor their learning progress along the way so that I can provide immediate feedback or make changes to my original plans. Plus, a lot of my assessments require students to engage with each other. I am always monitoring how they approach the learning and then make meaning of that learning. Oh, and how they get along." This last statement reflects Ms. Fitzgerald's intention of evaluating the skill, along with the will and thrill of her learners. Through her plan for evidence gathering, she can evaluate the dispositions her learners bring to the experience, along with their motivations.

Planning to Collect Evidence. In addition to planning the evidence to be gathered, we have to develop ways of collecting or organizing the evidence. Collecting an entrance ticket, exit ticket, or other student-generated artifacts is one way of obtaining the evidence. In addition, there needs to be a way of organizing evidence so that we can make meaning of student responses. Rich conversations, interactions, and actions that occur outside of tangible artifacts collected can also be used to determine impact.

Ms. Fitzgerald describes the importance of having a way to keep track of what is going on with her learners. "When learners are working in the laboratory, engaged in a discussion, or balancing equations, I need to make sure I jot down what I am seeing and hearing so that I can reference this evidence later on in the block or the next day. I use a record-keeping sheet that I keep close by during class." When we look at this record-keeping sheet, we see that Ms. Fitzgerald maintains her focus on the criteria for success, but broadens her view of evaluation to capture student learning beyond how they respond to an entrance ticket or exit ticket (see Table 5.2). "When I observe students engaging in academic discourse and working collaboratively with their peers, I get a feel for their buy-in and whether or not they see the value in what we are doing in class."

When we gather evidence through seeing and listening, we gain insight into learners' understanding, dispositions, and motivations. Collecting evidence through a handout limits our evaluation to whether or not they completed the handout, nothing more.

Anticipating Student Responses. The final aspect of planning for evaluation involves reflecting on our own content knowledge and pedagogical content knowledge. Ms. Fitzgerald has six years of experience and developed the expertise associated with the products of chemical reactions and how to teach this complex content to learners.

Table 5.2   Sample record-keeping sheet for collecting evidence

Criteria for Success	Observed Doing	Heard Saying	Saw Writing
I can **explain** the process for balancing equations.			
I can **predict** products for different chemical reactions.			
I can **justify** my prediction.			
I can **compare and contrast** products for synthesis, decomposition, single-replacement, double-replacement, and combustion reactions.			

Source: Adapted from Sweeney, D., & Harris, L. S. (2016). *Student-centered coaching: The moves.* Thousand Oaks, CA: Corwin.

"Having taught this before, I can look back and see where learners may struggle with predicting products. Although I make adjustments each year to respond to these potential pitfalls, I still spend time anticipating where my learners might need additional support or get stuck with this topic." We must set aside time before the lesson to think about how our learners might approach the day's learning experiences or tasks. What are possible misconceptions? What did the initial assessments tell me about my learners? Drawing from our diagnosis and discovery, anticipating student responses during the experience or task will help us focus on the most relevant evidence for evaluating impact. However, a word of caution is needed here. Anticipating student responses should be based on trends, patterns, and research on established misconceptions. In the end, learners will always surprise us with the way they approach learning. So, we should expect unexpected responses.

> Drawing from our diagnosis and discovery, anticipating student responses during the experience or task will help us focus on the most relevant evidence for evaluating impact.

Evaluating the Evidence

Evaluating the evidence guides us in making decisions about *what happens next* in our teaching and learning. We evaluate evidence by noticing the actions of our learners that reflect their understanding of the content and skills related to our learning intentions and success criteria. This brings us back to the process of teacher noticing introduced in Chapter 2. Just as initial assessments help us diagnose and discover where learners start out in the learning journey, assessments *as, for,* and *of* learning help us evaluate the success of implementation. These types of assessments (discussed in the upcoming pages) help us determine how successful we were in implementing what works best. From this gathered and collected evidence we must identify, recognize, and understand where students are now in their learning, make sense of what it means in relation to the interventions we decided to implement, and then decide where we go next. Let's look in on evidence generated from several students in Ms. Fitzgerald's chemistry class.

In the forthcoming discussion, to illustrate a significant idea about *evaluation*, we focus on specific learners for the first time. For this part of the DIIE model, we turn our attention to the observed learning outcomes of students. *Evaluation* turns our attention to the learners' progress in their skill, will, and thrill as a result of our teaching. Teachers who know how to implement what works best know when students are or are not learning and where to go next. This way of knowing comes from the evaluation of evidence.

Evaluation turns our attention to the learners' progress in their skill, will, and thrill as a result of our teaching.

The proceeding evidence about Zavian and Mikayla's learning should be evaluated based on where they are in their thinking (skill), their dispositions (will), and their motivations (thrill). For example, as Zavian and Mikayla engage in a discussion about the products of chemical reactions, Ms. Fitzgerald points out that "these two students went back and forth about the type of reaction which tells me that they were not clear on the essential characteristics of each type of reaction. They had many ideas, but could not articulate the relationship between the reactants and the type of chemical reaction." When evaluating students' thinking, Ms. Fitzgerald considers the questions presented in Table 5.3.

Ms. Fitzgerald recognizes what she observes, hears, and sees in writing as evidence for identifying where these two students are in their progress toward the day's success criteria. Determining where to go next involves moving students forward in uncovering relationships between different concepts, skills, and other content. Put differently, we should aim to move learners to the next level in their skill, while maintaining their will and thrill.

Two other students, Mariah and Jacob, engage in a discussion revolving around goal setting. Mariah can be overheard telling Jacob, "We need to spend some more time making sure we review the characteristics of each reaction and be able to explain why things happen the way they do with the reactants. That will make this go a bit easy. Predicting products, I mean." Much to Ms. Fitzgerald's delight, "These learners are motivated by what they don't know and have developed a self-directed goal to close this learning gap." This is likely different from learners in her class who simply raise their hand and immediately seek the help of Ms. Fitzgerald. Recognizing this difference across learners is valuable—it serves as evidence of will

Table 5.3 Questions for evaluating skill

1. Does the learner focus on single ideas or one way of thinking about the experience or task, not recognizing other aspects of the learning?
2. Does the learner work with multiple ideas, but does not yet see connections between those ideas?
3. Does the learner see relationships between different concepts, skills, and other content?
4. Does the learner apply ideas to different contexts?

Table 5.4 Questions for evaluating will and thrill

1. Does the learner recognize the gap between where he or she is and where he or she is going?
2. Does the learner set goals for closing this gap?
3. Does the learner apply learning strategies to close the gap?
4. Does the learner self-evaluate his or her progress in closing the gap?

and thrill as learners are making their dispositions and motivations visible to us. We must also acknowledge that what we observe, hear, and see in writing is evidence of will and thrill. When looking to notice the will and thrill of learning, Ms. Fitzgerald considers the questions presented in Table 5.4.

Where to next involves moving learners toward goal setting, the application of learning strategies, and self-evaluation. We should aim to move learners to the next level in will and thrill.

All of our students generate evidence of the learning. To ensure equity of access and opportunity to the most complex thinking, we must also ensure that evaluation plans include all learners. When scanning the learning environment, Ms. Fitzgerald samples the understanding of each student to ensure she knows where each one is in their progression toward the day's success criteria. She also begins to recognize trends or patterns in the observed learning outcomes for all of her students—outcomes that make their skill, will, and thrill visible. Her planning for evidence gathering and collecting heightens her awareness of all learners. "Several minutes into this part of the lesson, I noticed that I did not have any evidence of Josh and Brook's thinking. Planning out how I am going to monitor learning keeps me from overlooking those learners that I might assume get it or appear to get it simply because they finish first." Implementation of what works best should work for every student.

The Role of the Post-Assessments in Evaluation

Post-assessments are assessments *of* learning and also have an important role in evaluating our impact. If learning is about growth, post-assessments, or summative assessments, help us measure our impact over time. To capture this growth, teachers must provide an assessment that measures the same content, skills, and understandings that were measured in the initial assessment. For example, in a middle school English class, Ms. Dixon did not ask her students to rewrite the same argumentative essay for purposes of showing growth. Furthermore, simply using checks for understanding does not allow learners to pull their learning together through the planning and composing of an argumentative essay. Instead, she asked her learners to use the same skills and understanding on a different writing prompt. Although there are times when using the same pre-assessment as post-assessment is appropriate, this is not required for evaluating growth.

One way to evaluate the evidence of learning generated by assessments *of* learning is through an effect size. Just like the Visible Learning database, we can use an initial assessment and a post-assessment to calculate effect sizes for each learner and then an average effect size for groups of learners (e.g., an entire class or grade level). When the pre- and post-test data are available, the effect size can be determined. However, assessments *of* learning are similar to assessments *as* and *for* learning in that the evidence these assessments generate is not as important as what we do with those numbers. The evaluation of effect sizes should help us make decisions about where to go next. Ms. Dixon spends a lot of time evaluating the evidence generated by her post-assessments. "Not only do I want to see if I had an impact on their growth, I want to make sure my checks for understanding and my post-assessments tell a consistent story about my learners. Which learners made significant gains between the initial assessment and the post-assessment? Which learners did not make significant gains? Is this consistent with their checks for understanding?" Like Ms. Dixon, any teacher who measures his or her impact by looking at growth can still make intentional and purposeful decisions about where to go next with learners.

Collecting Evidence From Post-Assessments

> Any teacher who measures his or her impact by looking at growth can still make intentional and purposeful decisions about where to go next with learners.

Teachers can calculate effect sizes for their classes and individual students to determine the impact their teaching has on student learning. Student learning at the class level can be held to the same standard that researchers use: an effect size of at least 0.40. The process of calculating an effect size is fairly simple. For Ms. Dixon, as her learners submit their essays, she is interested in measuring her class's overall growth in writing as well as individual student growth. Table 5.5 contains the writing scores generated from the school district's common writing rubric. Ms. Dixon uses the 7-point rubric so that she can ensure that her learning intentions and success criteria align with what learners will experience throughout their secondary English and composition classes. The rubric includes descriptors for the elements of argumentative writing.

Table 5.5 Student writing scores

Name	Pre-Assessment	Post-Assessment	Individual Effect Size
Jakub	3.5	4.5	1.13
Lindsay	2.5	3	0.56
Mike	4	4.5	0.56
Darren	4	5.5	1.69
Leah	3.5	5	1.69
Mateus	4	6	2.26
Lydia	4	5	1.13
Karmen	5	6	1.13
Carly	4	3.5	−0.56
Ignacio	4	4.5	0.56
Jasmine	3.5	5	1.69
Amy	1.5	1.5	0.00
Shareen	3	3.5	0.56
Cris	3.5	5	1.69
Evelyn	5	5.5	0.56
Blair	3.5	4	0.56
Courtney	3	4	1.13
Dexter	4.5	5.5	1.13
Karen	3.5	5	1.69
Bruno	3.5	3	−0.56
Anna	3.5	5	1.69
Dana	4	5	1.13
Maya	5	5.5	0.56
Francis	4.5	6	1.69
Christian	4	6	2.26
Jared	3	5	2.26
Daneka	3.5	4	0.56

(Continued)

Table 5.5 (Continued)

Name	Pre-Assessment	Post-Assessment	Individual Effect Size
Brody	4.5	5.5	1.13
Adrian	4	5	1.13
Tim	3	4	1.13
Anthony	4	5	1.13
Class Average Score	3.74	4.69	
Class Standard Deviation for Each Assessment	0.74	1.03	
Average Standard Deviation	0.89		
Average Effect Size	1.08		

To calculate an effect size, you would first determine the average for the post-test and the average for the pre-test scores. It's easy to do this in an Excel spreadsheet, which is available as an online resource. Here's how:

- Type the students' names in one column.
- Type their scores for the pre- and post-assessments in other columns.
- Highlight the column with the pre-assessment scores and select the "average" tool and place the average at the bottom of that column.
- Do the same for the post-assessment column.

The next step in determining the effect size is to calculate standard deviation. Excel will do this as well*:

1. Type = STDEV.P and then select the student scores in the pre-assessment column again.
2. Do the same in the post-assessment column.
3. Subtract the pre-assessment from the post-assessment and then divide by the standard deviation.

Here's the formula:

$$\text{Effect Size} = \frac{\text{Average (post-assessment)} - \text{Average (pre-assessment)}}{\text{Average standard deviation or SD*}}$$

For Ms. Dixon's learners, the average pre-assessment score was 3.74. After two weeks of teaching and learning on argumentative writing, her learners increased their average writing score to 4.69. To determine the magnitude of this impact, Ms. Dixon will have to look beyond change in students' performance on the rubric. Average growth doesn't provide the evidence necessary for her to identify, recognize, and understand where students are now in their learning, make sense of what it means in relation to the interventions we decided to implement, and then decide where we go next. What she needs is relative growth from an effect size. When the effect size is calculated using the spreadsheet, it comes to 1.08, which is well above the threshold of 0.40 mentioned in the introduction of this book. Ms. Dixon now has evidence of growth that suggests her implementation of what works best has impacted the overall learning of her students. Once Ms. Dixon has the average effect size for the entire class, she can calculate the individual effect size for each student. This will allow her to see the growth of each individual's writing and notice trends or patterns in the learning growth for all of her students. The use of effect sizes when appropriate heightens her awareness of all learners.

QR Code 5.1 Calculate the effect size and view the Progress/Achievement Chart by downloading this Progress and Achievement Tool on the Visible Learning+ website

Evaluating the Evidence From Post-Assessments

Evaluating the evidence gathered from assessments *of* learning looks at the progress of learners. However, in the age of accountability, it is unrealistic to ignore achievement. Evaluating the evidence in terms of growth is more helpful in making decisions about "what, where, next" in students' learning. For Ms. Dixon, "I want to make sure that all of my learners are experiencing growth. There have been students that possess the skills and motivation to write from the very beginning of the year. But, I still need to have an impact on that learner's growth." Ms. Dixon is further evaluating her impact by not ignoring learners who meet achievement standards, but do not show growth with our learners. "It would be easy to ignore these learners. Their scores are fine. However, I am not having an impact on their learning." Ms. Dixon is correct, in most schools these learners are not addressed in evaluating our impact. But we are missing an opportunity to move all students' learning forward when we do not take both progress and achievement into our evaluation of evidence. One of the ways to visualize the relationship between progress and success is to construct a four-quadrant grid (see Figure 5.3).

The amount of progress students make scales left to right, whereas the overall level of achievement scales top to bottom. Of course, this requires that we have utilized an initial assessment to diagnose

Figure 5.3 Progress versus achievement grid

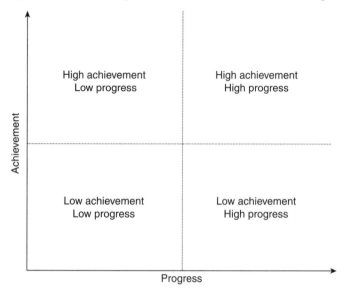

and discover where learners began in this journey, along with a post-assessment. A learner who has demonstrated high growth and met or exceeded benchmark scores would be located in the upper right-hand quadrant. For Ms. Fitzgerald and Ms. Dixon, this is evidence that they have had an impact on this learner; they implemented what works best, and the student is learning at high levels. The upper left-hand box represents those learners who have met or exceeded the benchmark scores, but have not demonstrated growth. Thus, there we have no measured impact on this learner. For example, this might be the student Ms. Dixon was worried about in the previous paragraph.

Learners represented in the two lower quadrants also provide important evidence in evaluating our impact. The lower right-hand quadrant includes students who are not yet meeting the benchmark scores, but are demonstrating above-average growth. For Ms. Fitzgerald and Ms. Dixon, this is evidence that they have had an impact on this learner; they implemented what works best, and the student is learning at high levels. Successive years of above-average growth will eventually lead to meeting or exceeding benchmark scores. Learning is happening! However, the students in the bottom left-hand quadrant need an immediate response. These learners are not meeting benchmark scores nor are they demonstrating growth. Again, the evidence these assessments generate is not as important as what we do with those numbers. In this situation, Ms. Dixon, Ms. Fitzgerald, or any teacher must immediately decide where to go next and provide compensatory or adaptive approaches to support these learners.

Fig 5.4 Growth versus achievement

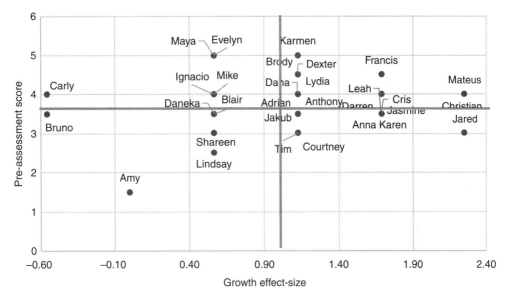

Let's have a look at the results of Ms. Dixon's class when their results are graphed according to achievement versus growth, shown in Figure 5.4.

While Carlo and Bruno began about average in the class, they showed the least growth, especially when compared to Mateus, Christian, and Jared, who started at the same place but made large spurts; May and Evelyn are among the most able students at pre-test but did not make much growth; Lindsay and Shareen started lower than average but Tim, Courtney, and Jared, who started somewhat similarly, made much greater growth—and so on. These questions beg answers, and hint to how Ms. Dixon needs to plan the next cycle of lessons. She should ask what led her to inspire the students with the greatest growth, no matter where they started. So often we focus on high and low achievers and ignore the more critical information about what students we have the greatest impact on in their growth toward the success criteria.

In the end, evaluation is about knowing and utilizing the skills needed to evaluate our impact on student learning through multiple methods of assessing. This includes assessment *as* learning, *for* learning, and *of* learning. Whether we are using checks for understanding or post-assessments, the evaluation of our impact should not be reduced to a score, mark, or grade. Instead, the power of evaluation lies in how we interpret the evidence and what we do with our knowledge of student progress in learning. Evaluation moves beyond *how we implement what works best*, and uses robust evidence generated by our learners to know, with confidence, whether *the implementation of what works best resulted in student*

Figure 5.5   Implementing what works best

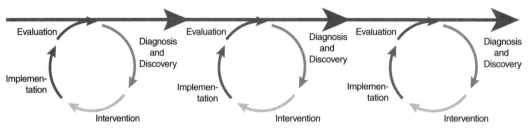

The DIIE model is how we close this gap. Great teaching can be designed, and when it's designed well, students learn more.

learning. Evaluation is not an end, but the starting point for making the next set of deliberate decisions about where to go next. In other words, back to and through the DIIE model.

Conclusion

We end right where we began with Oscar Vasquez and Katherine Meyer. The difference between these two teachers was not in their content knowledge, or their knowledge about teaching and learning. They did not lack good ideas in their planning for instruction or how to engage and motivate learners. The key difference between these two teachers was that Mr. Vasquez knew how to effectively implement what works best. He can take a good idea from potential to implementation. This set up the problem this book set out to solve: to close the gap between potential to implementation. What is worth reiterating is the fact that moving from potential to implementation is a necessary process in any learning environment—face-to-face, hybrid, and virtual. Whether seated in the kitchen or at a table in a kindergarten classroom, we have to diagnose and discover, select an intervention, implement that intervention, and continuously evaluate our impact. The platform by which this process occurs does not matter as much as the decisions we make as the teacher. In the end, we are still working to ensure that our learners are further along in their learning journey at the end of the day than they were at the start of the day, just because of time spent with us.

For Mr. Vasquez and all of the teachers featured in this book, they *implement what works best* by explicitly uncovering where our learners are in their learning journey, drawing what works best in teaching and learning from our professional knowledge base, and continuously evaluating the impact of our decisions on student learning. The results of that evaluation of impact take us right back to our understanding of where learners are *now* in their learning journey. The process starts all over again.

REFERENCES

Acala, L. (2018, September 8). My favorite no: Learning from mistakes. Retrieved from https://learn.teachingchannel.com/video/class-warm-up-routine

Ainsworth, L., & Donovan, K. (2019). *Rigorous curriculum design* (2nd ed.). Boston, MA: Houghton Mifflin Harcourt.

Antonetti, J., & Stice, T. (2018). *#Powerful task design: Rigorous and engaging tasks to level up instruction*. Thousand Oaks, CA: Corwin.

Australian Children's Education & Care Quality Authority. (2018, February). The environment as the 'third teacher'. *National Quality Standard: QA 3*. Retrieved from www.acecqa.gov.au

Ball, D. L., & Bass, H. (2009). With an eye on the mathematical horizon: Knowing mathematics for teaching to learners' mathematical futures. In M. Neubrand (Ed.), *Beitrage zum Mathematikunterricht* 2009: Vortrage auf der 43. Tagung für Didaktik der Mathematik vom 2.-6. Marz 2009 in Oldenburg (Bande 1 und 2, pp. 11–29). Munster, Germany: WTM-Verlag.

Beekes, R. (2010). *Etymological dictionary of Greek*. Leiden, Netherlands: Brill.

Berliner, D. C. (2001). Learning about and learning from expert teachers. *International Journal of Educational Research, 35(5),* 463–482.

Boaler, J. (2016). *Mathematical mindsets. Unleashing students' potential through creative math, inspiring messages and innovative teaching.* San Francisco, CA: Jossey-Bass.

Brophy. J. (1998). *Motivating students to learn.* New York, NY: McGraw-Hill.

Bustamante, V., & Almarode, J. (2020, April 6). Teaching and learning in the new normal. *Corwin Connect.* Retrieved from https://corwin-connect.com/2020/04/teaching-and-learning-in-the-new-normal/

Butler, R., (2017). Why choose teaching, and does it matter? In H. M. G. Watt, P. W. Richardson, & K. Smith (Eds.), *Global perspectives on teacher motivation* (pp. 377–388). Cambridge, UK: Cambridge University Press.

Cornelius-White, J. (2007). Learner-centered teacher-student relationships are effective: A meta-analysis. *Review of Educational Research*, *77*(1), 113–143.

Darling-Hammond, L., & Oakes, J. (2019). *Preparing teachers for deeper learning.* Harvard Education Press: Cambridge, MA.

Eccles, J. (2005). Subjective task value and the Eccles et al. model of achievement-related choices. In A. J. Elliot & C. S. Dweck (Eds.), *Handbook of competence and motivation* (pp. 105–121). New York, NY: Guilford.

Erickson, F. (2011). On noticing teacher noticing. In M. G. Sherin, V. R. Jacobs, & R. A. Philipp (Eds.), *Mathematics teacher noticing: Seeing through the teachers' eyes* (pp. 17–34). New York, NY: Routledge.

Fisher, D., & Frey, N. (2004). *Inclusive urban schools.* Baltimore, MD: Paul H. Brookes.

Fisher, D., Frey, N., & Hattie, J. (2016). *Visible learning for literacy.* Thousand Oaks, CA: Corwin.

Frey, N., Hattie, J., & Fisher, D. (2018). *Developing assessment-capable visible learners, grades K–12: Maximizing skill, will, and thrill.* Thousand Oaks, CA: Corwin.

Guskey, T. R. (2018). Does pre-assessment work? *Educational Leadership, 75(5),* 52–57.

Guskey, T. R., & McTighe, J. (2016). Pre-assessment: Promises and cautions. *Educational Leadership, 73(17).* 38–43.

Hattie, J., (2009). *Visible learning: A synthesis of over 800 meta-analyses relating to achievement.* New York, NY: Routledge.

Hattie, J., (2012). *Visible learning for teachers: Maximizing impact on learning.* New York, NY: Routledge.

Hattie, J., & Donoghue, G. M. (2016). Learning strategies: A synthesis and conceptual model. *NPJ Science of Learning, 1,* 1–13.

Hattie, J., & Zierer, K. (2018). *10 mindframes for visible learning: Teaching for success.* Thousand Oaks, CA: Corwin.

Hattie, J., & Zierer, K. (2019). *Visible learning insights.* New York, NY: Routledge.

Hockett, J. A., & Doubet, K. J., (2014). Turning on the lights: What pre-assessments can do. *Educational Leadership, 71*(4), 50–54.

Kahneman, D., & Tversky, A., Eds. (2000). *Choices, values, and frames.* New York, NY: Cambridge University Press.

Lauermann, L., Karabenick, S. A., Carpenter, R., & Kuusinen, C. (2017). Teacher motivation and professional commitment in the United States: The role of motivations for teaching, teacher self-efficacy and sense of professional responsibility. In H. M. G. Watt, P. W. Richardson, & K. Smith (Eds.), *Global perspectives on teacher motivation* (pp. 322–348). Cambridge, UK: Cambridge University Press.

Malaguzzi, L. (1984). *When the eye jumps over the wall: Narratives of the possible.* Regione Emilia Romagna, Comune di Reggio Emilia.

Marzano, R. J. (2017). *The new art and science of teaching.* Solution Tree Press: Bloomington, IN.

Nuthall, G., (2007). *The hidden lives of learners.* NZCER Press. Wellington, NZ.

Posner, G. (2004). *Analyzing the curriculum* (3rd ed.). McGraw-Hill: New York, NY.

Saphier, J., Haley-Speca, M. A., & Gower, R. (2018). *The skillful teacher* (7th ed.). Acton, MA: Research for Better Teaching, Inc.

Schoenfeld, A. H. (2011). Noticing matters. A lot. Now what?. In M. G. Sherin, V. R. Jacobs, & R. A. Philipp (Eds.), *Mathematics teacher noticing: Seeing through the teachers' eyes* (pp. 223–238). New York, NY: Routledge.

Sherin, M. G., Jacobs, V. R., & Philipp, R. A. (2011). Situating the study of teacher noticing. In M. G. Sherin, V. R. Jacobs, & R. A. Philipp (Eds.), *Mathematics teacher noticing: Seeing through the teachers' eyes* (pp. 3–13). New York, NY: Routledge.

Sparks, S. (2019, March 12). Why teacher-student relationships matter. *Education Week.* https://www.edweek.org/ew/articles/2019/03/13/why-teacher-student-relationships-matter.html

Strong, J. H. (2018). *Qualities of effective teachers* (3rd ed.). Alexandria, VA: ASCD.

Sweeney, D., & Harris, L. S. (2016). *Student-centered coaching: The moves.* Thousand Oaks, CA: Corwin.

Szidon, K., & Franzone, E. (2009). Task analysis. Madison, National Professional Development Center on Autism Spectrum Disorders, Waisman Center, University of Wisconsin.

Watt, H. M. G., & Richardson, P. W., (2007). Motivational factors influencing teaching as a career choice: Development and validation of the FIT-Choice scale. *Journal of Experimental Education, 75,* 167–202.

Watt, H. M. G., Richardson, P. W., & Smith, K. (2017). Why teach? How teachers' motivations matter around the world. In H. M. G. Watt, P. W. Richardson, & K. Smith (Eds.), *Global perspectives on teacher motivation* (pp. 1–21). Cambridge, UK: Cambridge University Press.

INDEX

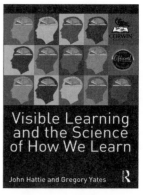

10 MINDFRAMES FOR VISIBLE LEARNING

10 MINDFRAMES FOR LEADERS

VISIBLE LEARNING FEEDBACK

DEVELOPING ASSESSMENT-CAPABLE VISIBLE LEARNERS, Grades K–12

VISIBLE LEARNING FOR LITERACY, Grades K–12

TEACHING LITERACY IN THE VISIBLE LEARNING CLASSROOM, Grades K–5, 6–12

VISIBLE LEARNING FOR MATHEMATICS, Grades K–12

TEACHING MATHEMATICS IN THE VISIBLE LEARNING CLASSROOM, Grades K–2, 3–5, 6–8, & High School

VISIBLE LEARNING FOR SCIENCE, Grades K–12

VISIBLE LEARNING FOR SOCIAL STUDIES, Grades K–12